TRANSITION
in Alabama

Reports of previous studies of the Council,

> *Water and Economic Growth*—1960
> *Flight From the Soil*—1958
> *Alabama Goes Industry Hunting*—1957
> *Skills For Progress*—1956
> *Alabama's Manufacturing Economy*—1955

may be obtained from

> The Alabama Business Research Council
> Box 6222
> University, Alabama

(Price: $1.00 each)

TRANSITION in Alabama

a study by the
ALABAMA BUSINESS RESEARCH COUNCIL

1962
UNIVERSITY OF ALABAMA PRESS

ALABAMA BUSINESS RESEARCH COUNCIL

The ALABAMA BUSINESS RESEARCH COUNCIL is composed of Alabama business executives and senior faculty members of the University of Alabama. It was formed in 1953 to study selected topics of interest and importance to the Alabama community.

The research studies are conducted by the members of the Research Committee in cooperation with the Faculty Advisory Committee. Through the latter the resources of the University are made available to the business executives named by their firms to the Research Committee.

The Advisory Committee, currently consisting of forty-seven top executives, acts in an advisory capacity, assures the financial support of the Alabama Business Research Council, and participates in planning the research program. A roster of members of the Alabama Business Research Council appears in the Appendix.

Published for the Alabama Business Research Council by
University of Alabama Press, Drawer 2877, University, Alabama
Copyright 1962 by University of Alabama
Printed and bound by Drake Printers
Library of Congress Catalog Card Number 62-19746

THIS BOOK IS DEDICATED TO LEE BIDGOOD, FOUNDER AND DEAN OF THE SCHOOL OF Commerce and Business Administration, University of Alabama, 1919-1954, in appreciation of his inspiration as Coördinator of the Research Committee and in recognition of his half-century contribution to the business community of Alabama and the nation.

Acknowledgments

To:

Mr. R. V. Miles, Jr., Vice President, Gulf States Paper Corporation, Tuscaloosa, Alabama, for a very extensive compilation of facts and figures on forestry in Alabama, including the production of wood, processing of it into various forms, data on forest management including tree farms, and much other useful information.

Mr. J. M. Stauffer, Chief, Division of Forestry, Alabama Department of Conservation, Montgomery, Alabama.

Mr. Robert A. Driscoll, Research Assistant, Institute of Life Insurance, New York, New York, for calculations of the rank of Alabama among the states in insurance in force and of the percentage of the nation's life insurance in force in Alabama, and for two printed pamphlets on life insurance.

Farm Journal for permission to quote.

Miss Alice Kingery, Business Librarian, and her staff for

helping obtain bibliographical information on a great many subjects.

Staff of the Bureau of Business Research for assistance of many kinds.

Mr. Merrill C. Lofton, Field Office Manager, U. S. Department of Commerce, Field Services, Atlanta, Georgia.

Mr. Ralph W. Roberts, State Registrar, Alabama State Department of Health, Bureau of Vital Statistics, Montgomery, Alabama.

Mr. Clifford W. Patton, Information Service, Federal Home Loan Bank Board, Washington, D. C.

At this place I cannot refrain from attempting to express my keen enjoyment in working with the Research Committee of the Alabama Business Research Council on the preparation of this book. It has proved to be an intellectual challenge and a very pleasant personal association.

Lee Bidgood
Research Coördinator

Alabama in Transition: Whither Bound?

THE ALABAMA BUSINESS RESEARCH COUNCIL HAS PUBLISHED FIVE research studies prior to this year. Each of the published studies centered attention on one important facet of the Alabama economy. In 1955 the Research Committee gathered basic data concerning the structure of manufacturing in the state. The result was publication of *Alabama's Manufacturing Economy*. In 1956 the study dealt with personnel engaged in manufacturing, finance, newspapers, and department stores. Emphasis was centered on top management, junior executive enlistment and training, and the working force of some of Alabama's leading firms. Data collected were incorporated in the ABRC publication, *Skills for Progress*. The following year, 1957, the ABRC published *Alabama Goes Industry Hunting*, a study which sought to evaluate the efficiency of organized efforts to expand Alabama's industrial-business base. As a result of the 1958 study and research concerning the changes in agriculture which affect industry and business in Alabama, the ABRC published *Flight From the Soil*. In 1960, with the publication of *Water and Economic Growth: A Study of Alabama and the Southeast*, the

Alabama Business Research Council added a monograph which stressed the availability of water as a basis for future expansion of the state's economy.

A common characteristic of the findings of these five dissimilar studies was change: the economy of Alabama is changing. This consistent presence of change in specific aspects of the state's economy—the expansion of industry; the proliferation of manufacturing activities; the keen searching out of new firms, plants, and industries; the increasing industrial and business contribution to the income of the people; the changing proportional distribution of wages, salaries, and investment resulting from shifts among industry groups; the effects of increasing total and per capita personal income on the development and expansion of markets—changes which were recognized in preceding studies, called for a broadly based study of Alabama in transition.

The major purpose of this study is to summarize and evaluate the changes which have characterized the Alabama economy over the last two decades and to take note of the general direction of these changes. Not all of the dramatic changes that have stimulated economic readjustments are considered in this publication.

Change generates change, creating a flow of interrelated innovations and adaptations. Twenty years of this process have brought about an economic revolution and created in Alabama an economy which contrasts sharply with that of two decades ago.

The readers of this publication will be impelled to conclude that Alabama is no longer a share-cropper, poverty-stricken, predominantly agricultural state.

Contents

ACKNOWLEDGMENTS	v
FOREWORD: Alabama in Transition: Whither Bound?	vii
INTRODUCTION: Economic Revolution in Alabama	1

PART I: PEOPLE AND THEIR RESOURCES

THE PEOPLE IN ALABAMA	15
Birth and Death Rates	18
Urban and Rural Distribution	21
Distribution by Counties	24
Households	26
Nonwhite and Negro Population	27
Age and Sex Characteristics	28
PERSONAL INCOME	31

SAVINGS	36
HOUSING	43

PART II: GREEN HILLS AND VALLEYS

AGRICULTURAL TRANSFORMATION	49
FORESTRY IN THE NEW ECONOMY	56

PART III: INDUSTRY AND BASIC SERVICES

FARM FIELDS TO FACTORY SITES	63
GROWTH IN BASIC SERVICES	72

PART IV: THE MARKETING STRUCTURE

WHOLESALE TRADE	83
RETAIL TRADE	88
HIGHLIGHTS OF THE STUDY	91
ALABAMA BUSINESS RESEARCH COUNCIL	100

Figures and Tables

FIGURE 1—BIRTH AND DEATH RATES, ALABAMA AND THE UNITED STATES, 1940 TO 1959 ... 19

TABLE 1—CHANGES IN DISTRIBUTION OF PERSONAL INCOME, BY MAJOR SOURCES, ALABAMA, 1939, 1949, AND 1959 ... 4

FIGURE 2—BIRTH AND DEATH RATES, WHITE AND NONWHITE, ALABAMA, 1940 TO 1960 ... 20

TABLE 2—IMPORTS BY COMMODITY GROUPS, MOBILE CUSTOMS DISTRICT, 1950 TO 1960 ... 8

FIGURE 3—TRENDS IN URBAN, RURAL AND TOTAL POPULATION, ALABAMA, 1830 TO 1960 ... 22

TABLE 3—URBAN AND RURAL POPULATION, ALABAMA, 1950 AND 1960 ... 23

FIGURE 4—CHANGES IN POPULATION BY COUNTIES, ALABAMA, 1940 TO 1960 ... 25

TABLE 4—SELECTED STATISTICS OF COMMERCIAL BANKS, ALABAMA AND THE UNITED STATES, 1940, 1950, AND 1960 ... 38

FIGURE 5	—CHANGES IN AGE AND SEX DISTRIBUTION OF WHITE AND NONWHITE POPULATION, ALABAMA, 1940 TO 1960	29
TABLE 5	—LIFE INSURANCE IN FORCE IN ALABAMA	39
FIGURE 6	—PER CAPITA PERSONAL INCOME, ALABAMA, 1940, 1950, AND 1960	32
TABLE 6	—SAVINGS IN SAVINGS AND LOAN ASSOCIATIONS, CREDIT UNIONS AND POSTAL SAVINGS, ALABAMA	41
FIGURE 7	—ALABAMA'S PERSONAL INCOME 6½ TIMES AS MUCH AS IT WAS TWENTY YEARS AGO	34
TABLE 7	—CASH RECEIPTS FROM FARM MARKETINGS, ALABAMA	53
FIGURE 8	—OWNER AND RENTER OCCUPIED HOUSING UNITS, ALABAMA, 1940, 1950, AND 1960	44
TABLE 8	—AVERAGE PRODUCTION OF FOREST PRODUCTS, ALABAMA, 1958-60 COMPARED TO 1952-54	61
FIGURE 9	—CHANGE IN CONDITION OF OCCUPIED HOUSING UNITS, ALABAMA, 1940, 1950, AND 1960	46
TABLE 9	—PERCENTAGE DISTRIBUTION OF VALUE ADDED BY MANUFACTURE, SELECTED COUNTY GROUPINGS, ALABAMA, 1939, 1947, 1954, AND 1958	69
FIGURE 10	—PERCENTAGE OF LAND IN FARMS, ALABAMA, 1920 TO 1959	51
TABLE 10	—RATIOS OF WHOLESALE TO RETAIL SALES, ALABAMA CITIES, 1939, 1948, 1954, AND 1958	85
FIGURE 11	—PRODUCTION OF LUMBER AND PULPWOOD, ALABAMA, 1946 TO 1960	60
TABLE 11	—WHOLESALING STRUCTURE, ALABAMA AND THE UNITED STATES, 1939, 1948, 1954, AND 1958	86

FIGURE 12—NUMBER OF EMPLOYEES, VALUE ADDED BY MANUFACTURE AND VALUE ADDED PER EMPLOYEE BY INDUSTRY GROUP, ALABAMA, 1947, 1954, AND 1958   67

TABLE 12—ALABAMA AS A PERCENTAGE OF UNITED STATES: RETAIL SALES, POPULATION, PERSONAL INCOME, AND PER CAPITA INCOME, SELECTED YEARS, 1939 TO 1960   88

TABLE 13—RETAIL TRADE, BY KIND OF BUSINESS GROUP, ALABAMA, AND PERCENTAGE DISTRIBUTION OF RETAIL TRADE, ALABAMA AND UNITED STATES, 1948 AND 1958   90

Economic Revolution in Alabama

THIS VOLUME IS A STUDY OF THE CHANGING ASPECTS OF THE ALAbama economy. Our field covers approximately two decades, with especial reference to the changes revealed by the censuses taken during the three years 1958 through 1960. We have found these changes to be so many and so great that we are constrained to give our readers prompt notice that an economic revolution has taken place in Alabama. The changes are more profound than any that have occurred here in more than a century.

First it seems fitting to call attention to the fact that the Cotton Economy, which came into Alabama at about the same time as statehood, has ended. Almost universal dependence on growing cotton for a living is a thing of the past. In 1959 only a trifling part, specifically about 1.5 per cent, of the income of the people of Alabama came from growing cotton.

Cotton had come to the head of the economy in Alabama on a wave of abundance. In the first third of the nineteenth century, when Eli Whitney, Daniel Pratt, the Alabama planters, and their slaves joined with the cotton mill men to revolutionize the production of textiles, they brought a clothing abundance previously unknown. It spread over most of the world.

Cotton came back to economic pre-eminence in Alabama after the great War Between the States. Still serving abundance under the control of free enterprise it survived even the still more terrible "Reconstruction."

The end of the Cotton Economy was foretold in the depression of the 1930's when it fell under the control of Washington planners operating under the theory of scarcity. The classic record is the picture of a ragged sharecropper, with his poor mule, plowing under his scanty crop of cotton in return for a Federal pittance. If free enterprise were to survive, most of the people in Alabama who were then growing cotton would have to find something better to do most of the time.

They have found better things to do.

There is a place in Alabama for cotton as a crop to be grown on suitable soil in large fields prepared, planted, cultivated, and harvested in modern fashion. There is no longer a place in Alabama for Cotton as in the phrases Cotton State, Cotton Belt, and King Cotton.

Not only is Alabama no longer a cotton farming state, it is not even an agricultural state. Twenty years ago farming produced about 15 per cent of the income of the people of Alabama. In 1959 farming yielded just 5.8 per cent of their income.

One third of all the Alabama farmers quit the soil between 1954 and 1959. Those who left included nearly half of all the tenant farmers in the state. There are only 32,000 farm tenants left in Alabama, 32,000 farm tenants in a state where there are 375,000 *rural* households.

Cotton not only does not lead the economy, it does not even lead farming in Alabama. It dropped from nearly three-fourths of the total farm product in 1924 to less than one-fourth in 1959. Livestock and its products made up over half of all the sales of agricultural products in 1959. This is a livestock state, to the extent that it is an agricultural state at all.

Alabama is not even a rural state. It is an urban state, already more urban than one-third of the other states, and gaining in urbanization faster than two-thirds of the other states.

Now that we have said our adieux to Ex-King Cotton, it is fitting time to end the tales about the mineral eminence of Alabama. To do this requires only the statement of the principal facts.

Alabama enjoys a substantial output of minerals—almost two hundred million dollars worth in 1959. This was 1.17 per cent of the United States total. Our share of the national income in that year was 1.21 per cent, so the state's economy as a whole did a little better than its mineral segment. Alabama ranked twenty-first among the states in order of mineral output. The principal minerals in order of value were coal, cement, stone, and iron ore.

Mineral production in this state increased a little in 1960. The top four minerals were the same as in 1959. The fifth was oil, the production of which has increased nearly ten-fold in ten years. Its value, disclosed for the first time in several years, came to nearly $22,000,000.

How the idea originated that Alabama ever was a state of outstanding importance in the mineral industries is not clear. But it did produce much more coal and iron ore some decades ago than it does now. Production of coal reached its peak in 1926. It was 40 per cent lower in 1959. Shipments of iron ore came to a peak in 1942, under pressure of war demand. They were 48 per cent lower in 1959.

At this point we call attention to the fact that agriculture and mineral production combined account for about 10 per cent of the income of the people in Alabama. This means that the state's economy is of a highly advanced type. Only a tenth of the people's living comes from agrarian and extractive activities, nine-tenths from pursuits developed later in the course of economic history. The advanced economy is always stronger and richer than an extractive or agricultural system. It is a much better and bigger market. The Alabama production system is advanced enough now to furnish enough money for the consumers of the state to buy almost any kind of service or product.

TABLE 1. CHANGES IN DISTRIBUTION OF PERSONAL INCOME, BY MAJOR SOURCES, ALABAMA, 1939, 1949, AND 1959

Source of personal income	1939		1949		1959		Per cent change		
	Millions of dollars	Per cent distribution	Millions of dollars	Per cent distribution	Millions of dollars	Per cent distribution	1939-49	1949-59	1939-59
TOTAL PERSONAL INCOME	704	100.0	2,429	100.0	4,607	100.0	245.0	89.7	554.4
Wage and salary disbursements	441	62.6	1,500	61.8	3,112	67.5	240.1	107.5	605.7
Farms	10	1.4	36	1.5	32	.7	260.0	−11.1	220.0
Mining	27	3.9	69	2.8	62	1.3	155.6	−10.1	129.6
Coal mining	19	2.8	46	1.9	40	.9	142.1	−13.0	110.5
Crude petroleum and natural gas	......	......	(1)	(2)	2	(2)	......	......	......
Mining and quarrying, except fuel	8	1.1	22	.9	20	.4	175.0	−9.1	150.0
Contract construction	13	1.8	66	2.8	166	3.6	407.7	151.5	1,176.9
Manufacturing	125	17.9	480	19.8	968	21.0	284.0	101.7	674.4
Wholesale and retail trade	61	8.7	247	10.2	489	10.6	304.9	98.0	701.6
Finance, insurance, and real estate	13	1.8	52	2.1	134	2.9	300.0	157.7	930.8
Banking and other finances	6	.9	17	.7	44	1.0	183.3	158.8	633.3
Insurance and real estate	6	.9	35	1.4	90	1.9	483.3	157.1	1,400.0
Transportation	36	5.1	120	5.0	146	3.2	233.3	21.7	305.6
Railroads	26	3.7	71	2.9	65	1.4	173.1	−8.5	150.0
Highway freight and warehousing	3	.4	11	.5	44	1.0	266.7	300.0	1,366.7
Other transportation	7	1.0	39	1.6	37	.8	457.1	−5.1	428.6
Communications and public utilities	12	1.7	40	1.6	92	2.0	233.3	130.0	666.7
Telephone, telegraph, and other communications	4	.6	18	.7	43	.9	350.0	138.9	975.0
Electric, gas, and other public utilities	8	1.1	22	.9	49	1.1	175.0	122.7	512.5

(continued)

TABLE 1 (continued)

Source of personal income	1939		1949		1959		Per cent change		
	Millions of dollars	Per cent distribution	Millions of dollars	Per cent distribution	Millions of dollars	Per cent distribution	1939-49	1949-59	1939-59
Services	44	6.2	144	5.9	284	6.2	227.3	97.2	545.5
Hotels and other lodging places	2	.2	5	.2	10	.2	150.0	100.0	400.0
Personal services and private households	26	3.7	81	3.3	110	2.4	211.5	35.8	323.1
Business and repair services	4	.5	9	.4	55	1.2	125.0	511.1	1,275.0
Amusement and recreation	2	.3	7	.3	9	.2	250.0	28.6	350.0
Professional, social, and related services	11	1.5	42	1.7	101	2.2	281.8	140.5	818.2
Government	97	13.8	243	10.0	735	16.0	150.5	202.5	657.7
Federal, civilian	55	7.7	94	3.9	318	6.9	70.9	238.3	478.2
Federal, military	2	.3	30	1.2	118	2.6	1,400.0	293.3	5,800.0
State and local	41	5.8	119	4.9	299	6.5	190.2	151.3	629.3
Other industries	2	.3	3	.1	4	.1	50.0	33.3	100.0
Other labor income	5	.7	33	1.4	124	2.7	560.0	275.8	2,380.0
Proprietors' income	166	23.7	505	20.8	687	14.9	204.2	36.0	313.9
Farm	95	13.5	250	10.3	240	5.2	163.2	— 4.0	152.6
Nonfarm	72	10.2	255	10.5	447	9.7	254.2	75.3	520.8
Property income	73	10.4	212	8.7	406	8.8	190.4	91.5	456.2
Transfer payments	25	3.6	210	8.6	381	8.3	740.0	81.4	1,424.0
Less: Personal contributions for social insurance	7	1.0	31	1.3	104	2.3	342.9	235.5	1,385.7

(1) Less than $500,000.   (2) Less than 0.1%.

Sources: 1939 and 1949, *Personal Income by States Since 1929*, a supplement to the *Survey of Current Business*, 1956; 1959, *Survey of Current Business*, August, 1960.

Let us particularly observe that recent changes in the farm picture have made the consumer aspect of the farm market practically indistinguishable from the urban market for consumer goods and services. The diet and dress are urban in type. Cars and homes and all the other things that people have are pretty much alike too. But in the country you will now see more, many more, empty houses rotting down. It is a pity they could not be towed off like old cars. This is evidence that a substantial portion of the farm market has now moved to the city and become urban market. Despite this movement, farmers have become a better market because a larger total agricultural income now goes to a sharply reduced number of people.

In income distribution, Alabama's is a wage-earning economy. It was a wage-earning economy even at the beginning of our period in 1939. Wages, salaries, and fringe benefits then accounted for nearly two-thirds of the personal income of the state's people. But by 1959 this share had grown to more than 70 per cent. Although proprietors' income had grown more than three-fold, its share of the total fell from nearly one-fourth in 1939 to about one-seventh in 1959. Property income was more than one-tenth of all personal income in 1939 and only one-eleventh in 1959. The consumer market in Alabama is dominated by the purchases of people who receive wages and salaries.

Who pays these salaries and wages? Private enterprise and government. Businesses: wholesale and retail trade; finance, insurance, and real estate; transportation; communications, and public utilities; services; and the like pay the largest part—about 37 per cent. Contract construction and manufacturing pay out almost as much—another 36 per cent; farms and mines 3 per cent; government 24 per cent, or almost one-fourth. Remember, this is just wages and salaries, as shown in Table 1. We are not including proprietors' and property income, or transfer payments.

Government's share of the salary and wage payments in Alabama increased by 7 per cent during the period of our study. Although public payrolls have been outgrowing private payrolls in our state, as elsewhere, the industrial market in Alabama

ECONOMIC REVOLUTION IN ALABAMA 7

remains largely a private enterprise market.

Businesses have done well as payroll makers in Alabama, too. Transportation, to be sure, has lost ground heavily, due to the fading importance of the railroads. The services group pays out about the same proportion of all salaries and wages that it did in 1939. So also do communications and public utilities as a group. Communications have increased their payout nicely, due, we think, to automation.

The finance, insurance, and real estate group has increased the importance of its position as a source of salary and wage payments by nearly 50 per cent since 1939. This, we think, is an especially healthy development; the people of Alabama are keeping and using a lot more of the money they make. Contract construction increased its share of the wage-salary distribution by 80 per cent between 1939 and 1959.

Manufacturing's gain of 10 per cent is not so startling. Factory production did not increase in Alabama as fast between the last two censuses of manufactures as in the period prior to 1950. That was the period covered by the Alabama Business Research Council's report, *Alabama's Manufacturing Economy*. The last few years have been marked by recession in some lines of manufacturing, progress in more. The net result has been good but over-all growth has been less spectacular. In general there has been a shift from industries with low value added by manufacture to industries with higher value added. Diversification has increased greatly. For example, lumber, a low value-added industry, has dropped from third to ninth place. Twenty years ago the top three industries turned out 60 per cent of all manufactured products in Alabama. Now they turn out less than half. Also, it takes seven industries to account for 70 per cent of the output. Manufacturing is well diversified in Alabama now. The industrial market is not only larger in volume but embraces many more products.

A class of products that is very important in the Alabama industrial market is the imports. To many people imports through a Gulf port has meant just bananas. But in 1960, half

TABLE 2. IMPORTS BY COMMODITY GROUPS, MOBILE CUSTOMS DISTRICT, 1950 TO 1960
(thousands of dollars)

Commodity group	1950	1951	1952	1953	1954	1955	1956	1957	1958	1959	1960
TOTAL IMPORTS	48,494	45,540	60,557	75,526	81,974	77,307	85,079	117,809	101,633	121,655	127,385
Meat, other than fresh or frozen	340	865	391	159	19	75		32	23	56	51
Fish and shellfish	9	111	6	423	1,311	908	666	623	783	1,803	1,615
Animal products, inedible, n.e.c.	28	35	28	7	602	445	653	1,370	1,163	1,568	78
Vegetable food products, except bananas	409	1,768	1,946	2,672	2,021	745	1,131	1,150	1,654	1,680	2,657
Bananas	5,092	5,768	4,981	4,923	6,015	6,893	6,546	6,805	6,292	6,484	7,008
Rubber, crude, and allied gums	11,079	1,770	5,669	9,230	9,175	15,596	8,986	11,903	5,400	8,224	9,897
Molasses, inedible	279	1,135	2,657	920	1,009	1,028	1,180	1,437	1,384	2,029	1,990
Sisal, henequen, jute, unmanufactured			840	2,708	4	470	275	1,016	1,886	1,785	2,224
Burlap and jute bagging	25	6	1,155	797	865	1,012	1,832	1,740	688	541	1,224
Logs	1	40	99	222	152	155	527	395	521	538	477
Wood containers; cooperage (except empty barrels); plywood, veneer			70	219	156	199	232	186	150	811	711
Woodpulp						4	3		441	1,273	2,185
Standard newsprint paper	2,339	3,098	3,606	4,208	4,041	3,529	3,514	3,423	3,221	3,585	3,284
Petroleum, crude	535	1,219	1,400	1,606	2,130	1,814	2,040	2,705	1,286	170	364
Residual fuel oil (including bunker oil)										220	2,540
Petroleum asphalt and products							75	437	1,904	1,736	1,618
Petroleum products, n.e.c.									284	543	427
Glass and glass products; brick and tile; clay products, n.e.c.; nonmetallic minerals and manufactures, n.e.c.	102	122	35	72	54	81	289	276	440	533	633
Iron ore and concentrates	2,562	3,641	6,051	7,041	13,485	11,270	14,727	19,434	21,734	24,391	22,996

(continued)

TABLE 2 (continued)

Commodity group	1950	1951	1952	1953	1954	1955	1956	1957	1958	1959	1960
Pig iron and scrap	484	637	......	693	7	......	......	......	......	1,315	......
Iron and steel products; castings; tools; household; pipe, tubing; rolled and finished steelmill products	745	3,450	1,801	2,303	922	734	2,808	4,431	3,747	11,752	10,054
Manganese, including ferromanganese	3,666	1,857	4,679	5,086	4,322	4,248	6,807	12,580	10,594	8,532	12,709
Chrome, including ferrochrome	17	......	......	1,433	......	777	3,337	9,197	3,368	3,035	1,926
Aluminum ores, concentrates, and scrap	10,029	10,516	11,727	14,150	14,608	14,639	19,129	21,791	17,088	18,423	19,837
Refined copper in crude forms; copper, semifabricated	1,806	3,051	5,188	2,750	10,747	311	320	66	800	300	68
Lead ores, concentrates, and scrap; lead and leadbase alloys in crude form	......	154	......	18	149	308	714	1,083	1,923	1,142	95
Tin metal in crude and semifabricated forms	3,785	848	1,352	4,031	1,718	4,208	1,661	6,860	3,838	5,093	6,662
Zinc ore, concentrates, and scrap	......	......	......	......	......	......	171	995	1,892	884	145
Automobiles, trucks, and busses; parts	......	47	......	......	33	15	37	1,444	1,623	2,882	2,947
Other machinery and vehicles	19	7	114	416	813	227	220	471	1,433	1,034	973
Benzol or benzene	......	......	......	......	......	......	......	......	......	1,379	2,067
Coal-tar products	390	353	544	483	257	198	......	12	52	30	1
Nitrogenous fertilizers and materials	4,111	3,597	3,924	7,316	6,783	6,377	4,987	4,849	4,656	5,415	3,840
Other commodities	642	1,445	2,294	1,640	576	1,041	2,212	1,098	1,365	2,469	4,082

Source: Bureau of Business Research, University of Alabama.

the imports of the Mobile Customs District—$64,000,000 worth—consisted of ores and metals. Ranked by quantity they were: iron ore, aluminum ores, manganese, tin, chrome, zinc, lead, and copper.

Alabama's great primary metals industry, its foremost manufacturing activity, depends for its prosperity, almost for its very existence, upon these imports and other outside supplies. The Mobile alumina plant is supplied with bauxite from Surinam. The Listerhill aluminum smelter gets its alumina from the plants at Hurricane Creek, Arkansas, and La Quinta, Texas. Bauxite for these plants in turn comes from Arkansas, British Guiana, Haiti, and Jamaica.

Iron ore, on the other hand, exists in very considerable quantities in Alabama. But nearly all of it has such a low iron content that it appears doubtful that any great quantity of it could be smelted profitably in competition with iron and steel from other states today, were it not for availability of richer ores for blending. These are received through the Port of Mobile in large quantities annually.

Another $20,000,000 of the Mobile imports in 1960 consisted of non-metallic materials used by Alabama industry. A single example will suffice: the $10,000,000 worth of rubber used by the tire plants in Gadsden and Tuscaloosa.

The contribution of the Port of Mobile to the development of Alabama's economy causes this facility to rank high among the state's resources. And it has been well developed. We do not neglect or underrate any of the other transportation facilities but call especial attention to this gateway to the outer world.

This appears to be a suitable time at which to remark that the newest, most profitable, and fastest growing type of agricultural development in Alabama—the production of livestock, especially broilers—resembles manufacturing such as we have described. The farmers use grain brought in from the Midwest to feed their animals, turning the grain into meat or other livestock products rapidly and scientifically.

All of these operations are alike in that we have in Alabama some special advantages in the operation undertaken: established markets, technical know-how, climatic advantage, transportation, especially skilled and adaptable labor, available facilities, power, certain of the raw materials and intermediate elements. The enterprisers look around, locate whatever else is needed for a successful operation, and bring it from abroad or from sister states.

This growing entrepreneurial activity is another very important aspect of the Alabama economy which now can be correctly described as an advanced one.

Only one of the great basic socio-economic truths about Alabama that have tended to distinguish its economy from the nation's remains valid, but it has been modified. This is that the Negro population is unusually large in number and high in percentage. The number of white people has increased substantially in the last twenty years and their percentage has risen from 65 to 70. Over the same twenty years the number of Negroes has remained virtually the same. There are only seven states in the union whose Negro population has not grown faster than Alabama's during the first half of this century. Yet there are still only six states, two northern and four southern, which at present have larger Negro populations than Alabama. Alabama is more old-timey in this respect than any other.

Many additional facts about the Alabama economy are included in this book but are not briefed here. We have told enough to establish that revolutionary changes have taken place. A new economy has evolved.

What do we consider the principal feature of this new economy? We consider its likeness to the economy of the nation as a whole to be its leading feature. Some social scientists think that the nation is growing more homogeneous throughout. Certainly the ways of making a living, the manner of living, and the standard of living in Alabama have become more like the national pattern.

Since we find the state's economy as a whole more and more like the nation's, we should also find the Alabama market to be more like the national market. We do so find it.

Many other types of data are included in this volume, but let us conclude our quick look at the economic revolution in Alabama with an appraisal of income. Everyone knows that in this century the huge income of the American people has become one of the wonders of the world. Its growth shows no signs of lessening.

Since 1929 the United States Department of Commerce has furnished annually reliable income figures for the people of each of the states. Every American state is a very rich area when viewed against the background of world economic conditions. But among themselves the states differ widely. There is a great deal of regularity in the sequence which they follow from year to year. Alabama has always been a low income state. When the first state income data were computed in 1929, it was fourth from the bottom; it is still fourth from the bottom. The states below it were the same in 1929 and in 1959.

Yet there have been great changes. What has happened is that all the states have moved closer together, nearer the national average. For example, the state with the largest per capita income in 1939 was Delaware. Alabama's was only about a fourth that size. Delaware's was also the biggest in 1959, and Alabama's had risen to about half its size.

Another way to see what has happened is to compare Alabama's per capita income with the nation's. Alabama's figure was less than half (46 per cent) of the nation's in 1929 and about two thirds (65 per cent) in 1959. Nearly all of this climb was made during the twenty-year period of our study. In 1940 Alabama's per capita income was still only 47 per cent of the national figure.

To gain on a richer state and on the nation, a poorer state must increase its income faster than they do. Since all of our states have made impressive gains in income, almost every year in recent years, the closing of the gap between state incomes is impressive testimony to the fact that the state economies are becoming more like the national economy.

We do not need to stop with the inference of a very rapid growth of income in Alabama. We can draw the figures from the publications of the Office of Business Economics in the United States Department of Commerce. From 1940 to 1960 per capita personal income grew faster in only two states than in Alabama. From 1940 to 1950 per capita income had grown faster in nine states, but from 1950 to 1960 the rate of growth in Alabama was the highest in the nation.

As compared with its sister states, Alabama is both a low state and a growth state in per capita income. Both facts are important from a market standpoint. Which is more significant must be regarded as a matter of opinion.

The series of studies by the Alabama Business Research Council have described some of the economic trends which have caused these income developments. More economic changes are narrated and analyzed in this volume.

A final reflection:

> The sweeping changes in the economic and social life of Alabama, set forth in this and other publications of the ABRC, especially *Alabama's Manufacturing Economy* and *Flight From the Soil*, resulted from individual decisions to an extent reminiscent of the eighteenth and early nineteenth centuries. People, high and low, rich, poor, and especially very poor, used their freedom of action to better their condition.

PART I: PEOPLE AND THEIR RESOURCES

The People in Alabama

IN THE FRONTIER PERIOD OF DEVELOPMENT OF ANY GEOGRAPHIC AREA there is a net inflow of people. This inflow may extend over a short or a long period of time, depending upon the balance between the rate of development of employment opportunities and the rate of natural increase of the population.

The point in time when a net inflow of population born elsewhere turns into a net outflow of native-born population may not mark the end of the frontier period, but it does mark the change from an excess of employment opportunities to an excess of native-born people.

The turning point between net inflow of people born elsewhere and the net outflow of native-born population for Alabama came between 1870 and 1880. By April 1, 1940, the date of the census of population for that year, there had been a net outflow of 488,000 native-born Alabamians who were then living in some other state. For every 100 people living in Alabama as of that date, 17 people who were born in Alabama were living in other states and more than half of these people (54 per cent) were white. By April 1, 1950, there had been a net outflow of

1,032,000 native-born Alabamians who were then living in other states. For every 100 people living in Alabama as of that date, 34 who were born in Alabama were living in other states and 61 per cent of these were white.

Unfortunately, more recent figures on outflow of native-born population will not be available for some months when special analyses are made of data collected in the 1960 census of population; however, the U. S. Bureau of the Census has prepared estimates of net total migration, by states, for the decades 1940 to 1950 and 1950 to 1960. Although these figures are aggregates of all movement into and out of Alabama, whether born here or not, they are indicative of the outflow of native-born persons since that group comprises the bulk of the total movement.

Because of a high birth rate and a low death rate, Alabama has produced more people, proportionately, than has the United States as a whole during the past several decades. As a consequence of these high birth rates and low death rates, the natural increase of population in Alabama has amounted to approximately 1,140,000 persons in the two decades since 1940. However, the net increase in population fell far short of this figure because many people did not stay in the state where they were born. Because of the movement of people to and from the state, Alabama suffered a net loss of 710,000 residents in the period 1940 to 1960, according to estimates by the Bureau of the Census.

Even after this heavy loss by net out-migration, there was still a net increase which raised the population from 2,832,961 in 1940 to 3,061,743 in 1950, and to 3,266,740 in 1960. This is an increase of more than 15 per cent, or nearly 434,000 persons for the twenty-year period. At the same time, the population of the United States increased at a rate nearly two and one-third times that for Alabama.

As long as there is an excess of people over job opportunities many of the people will move to other parts of the country where employment opportunities appear to be greater. It has often been said that the solution to an imbalance between people and job opportunities in an area is to have more people leave

THE PEOPLE IN ALABAMA

the area. That is only one way of looking at it. Another way, and a more profitable one in the long run, is to bring the job opportunities to people where they are.

The two major benefits of bringing the jobs to the people, in addition to the better utilization of available manpower, are that people are likely to be better socially adjusted when employed in the area in which they grow up and that further concentration of population in already congested areas is reduced.

As will be shown in the later portions of this study, there has been marked improvement in employment opportunities in Alabama and in the income of its people over the past two decades. As this trend continues into the future, more and more of those who otherwise would migrate will remain in the state to become producers and consumers in the Alabama market.

It is interesting to reflect upon what the population picture would have been had there been no net migration to or from Alabama between 1940 and 1960. Had the persons who moved from the state remained "at home," Alabama's population would have increased 40 per cent, rather than 15 per cent; a rate of growth 14 per cent greater than that for the United States. Further, Alabama's percentage of the nation's population in 1960 would have been 2.23 instead of 1.83.

What would it have meant to the economy of Alabama had it been possible to retain the seven hundred and ten thousand people lost from its population? By providing new job opportunities and employing the workers among them as effectively as the average of those who stayed, production in Alabama in 1960 would have increased by more than 20 per cent; retail sales would have been some half a billion dollars more than they were; and service sales, construction activity, professional services, transportation, and all other business activity would have been increased proportionately.

This situation is significant for producers and marketers of goods and services in the light of current trends of economic development in Alabama. Industry locating in Alabama can look forward to a greater than national rate of increase both in available manpower and in the market for consumer goods.

BIRTH AND DEATH RATES

During the decade of the forties, the average birth rate in Alabama exceeded that for the United States by nearly seven births per thousand population. Since 1948 the birth rate in the United States has been stable at about 25 births per thousand population annually, whereas the birth rate in Alabama has declined from a high of 31.9 per thousand in 1947 to 25.7 in 1959. Birth rates for Alabama and the United States for the years 1940 to 1959 are shown in Figure 1.

The differential between the death rates in Alabama and the United States also has narrowed over the past two decades. This also is illustrated in Figure 1. Alabama's average rate of 9.2 deaths per thousand population in the forties was 1.1 below the United States average. Although Alabama's rate fell to an average of 8.9 deaths per thousand population in the fifties, the United States death rate declined more rapidly so that the Alabama average was only 0.6 below the United States average for that decade.

Like the total birth rate, both the white and the nonwhite birth rates were higher in Alabama than in the nation for more than half of the twenty-year period studied. Since 1954 the reverse has been true; but, because of the greater proportion of nonwhite population in Alabama and the substantially higher nonwhite birth rate, Alabama's total birth rate continued to be higher than the birth rate for the United States.

Figure 2 shows how the nonwhite birth rate in Alabama has increased relative to the white birth rate. Since 1940 the nonwhite birth rate has ranged from 5 to 43 per cent (an average of 26 per cent) greater than the white birth rate. In 1959 the nonwhite birth rate was about 23 per cent larger than it had been in 1940; whereas the white birth rate was only about 5 per cent higher. In general, there was an increase in both white

FIGURE I
BIRTH AND DEATH RATES ALABAMA AND THE UNITED STATES 1940 TO 1959

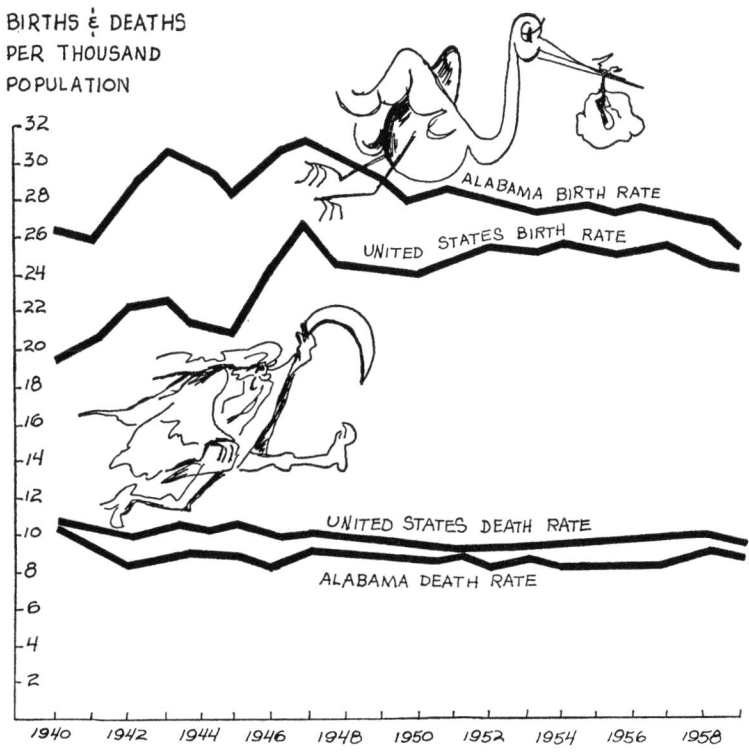

Source: Vital Statistics of the United States, National Office of Vital Statistics.

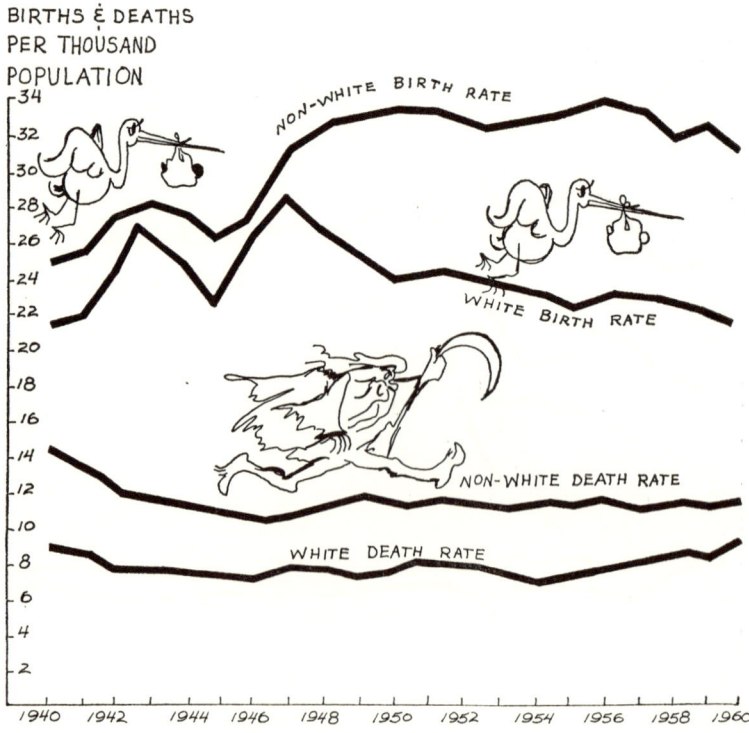

THE PEOPLE IN ALABAMA   21

and nonwhite birth rates during the 1940's and a decline during the following decade.

An examination of white and nonwhite death rates, presented in Figure 2, reveals a somewhat different pattern. During the twenty years under consideration, the white death rate in Alabama has been consistently lower than the national figure. The nonwhite death rate, on the other hand, was less than the national rate only for the period from 1941 to 1948. Since then the nonwhite death rate has been slightly higher in Alabama than in the nation, but not enough higher to raise the Alabama total death rate above that of the United States in any year.

URBAN AND RURAL DISTRIBUTION

Important changes also have occurred in the urban-rural distribution of the population over the past two decades. The decline of rural population as pointed out by the Alabama Business Research Council's earlier study, *Flight From the Soil*, has continued until it can be reported that Alabama is now an urban state with more than half of its people living in densely settled areas. Twenty years ago Alabama's population was about 70 per cent rural, but in 1960, by the same definition[1], it was only 48 per cent rural. These shifts in urban and rural population are shown in Figure 3, which is constructed on semi-logarithmic grid to emphasize the rate of change in population which is indicated by the steepness of slope of the lines connecting the plotted points. The steeper the rise or fall of these lines, the greater the ratio of increase or decrease from point to point.

Furthermore, Alabama is rapidly becoming urbanized. Population in urban territory increased nearly 34 per cent from 1950 to 1960 in contrast with the less than seven per cent increase in total population. Alabama ranked eighteenth among the states in rate of urban growth from 1950 to 1960, rising from thirty-

[1] The Census definition of urban and rural was changed in 1960. By the new definition Alabama was 45 per cent rural in 1960 and 56 per cent in 1950. Comparable figures are not available for 1940.

FIGURE 3

TRENDS IN URBAN, RURAL, & TOTAL POPULATION, ALABAMA 1830 TO 1960

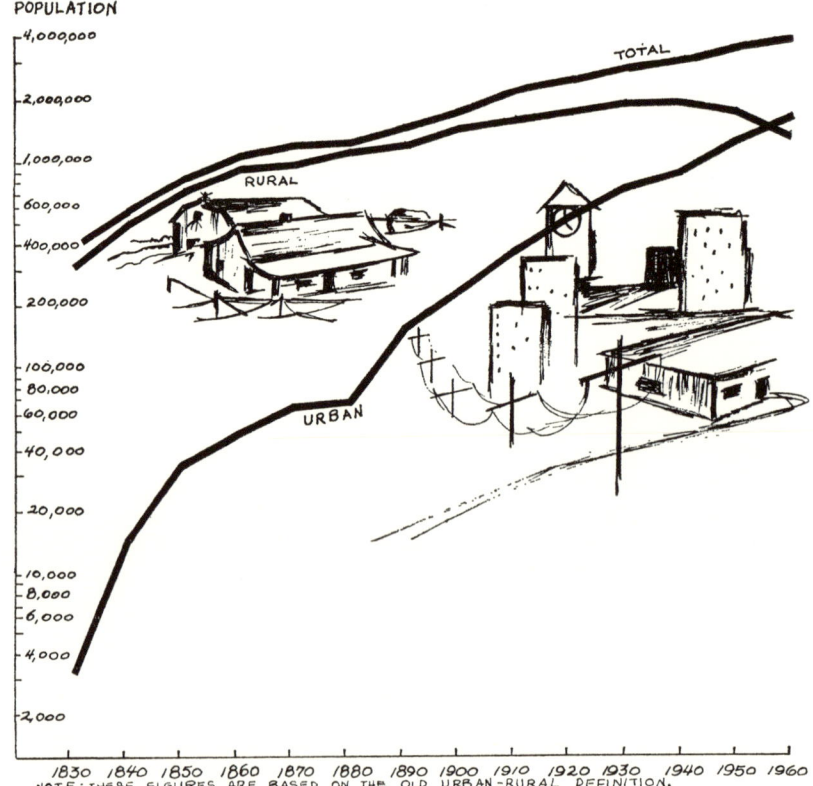

Source: U. S. Census of Population, 1960, Alabama, Number of Inhabitants, PC(1)-2A.

THE PEOPLE IN ALABAMA 23

fifth to thirty-second place in degree of urbanization.

In 1960 36 per cent of Alabama's population lived in seven urbanized areas. The six central cities,[2] hubs of the urbanized areas, held more than one-fourth (27 per cent) of its people.

TABLE 3. URBAN AND RURAL POPULATION, ALABAMA
1950 AND 1960 (New definition)

	1950		1960	
	Number	Per cent of total	Number	Per cent of total
Total population	3,061,743	100.0	3,266,740	100.0
Change from previous census	....		+ 6.7%	
Urban territory:				
Number of urban places	88		112	
Change from previous census	....		+27.3%	
Population in urban territory	1,340,937	43.8	1,791,721	54.8
Change from previous census	....		+33.6%	
Rural territory:				
Population in rural territory	1,720,806	56.2	1,475,019	45.2
Change from previous census	....		—14.3%	

Source: *U. S. Census of Population,* 1960. Number of Inhabitants, Alabama. Final Report PC (1)-2A.

There were twelve all-rural counties in 1960; there had been eighteen in 1950, and according to the old definition, twenty-six in 1940. Of the forty-nine counties with urban population in 1950, all save three had greater numbers of urban residents in 1960. The rate of increase from 1950 to 1960 was high in most of these counties. Fourteen counties increased by more than 50 per cent; only six counties did not increase in urban population by as much as 10 per cent. The median rate of urban increase by counties was just over 30 per cent. The increase of urban population in the state as a whole was nearly 34 per cent.

[2] One urbanized area in Alabama, Phenix City, centers on Columbus, Georgia.

All counties in Alabama have rural inhabitants, but sixty-two counties had fewer rural inhabitants in 1960 than in 1950. Rural population decreased less than 10 per cent in fifteen counties; in twenty-seven counties the decrease was between 20 and 46 per cent. There were only five counties in which rural population increased. The net effect was a reduction of a little more than 14 per cent in the rural population of the state.

DISTRIBUTION BY COUNTIES

Significant changes in the distribution of population by counties are illustrated in Figure 4.

Twenty-one of Alabama's sixty-seven counties recorded increases in population totaling nearly 665,000 persons. Two counties, Jefferson and Mobile, accounted for 52 per cent of this increase. Fifteen of the twenty-one counties experienced an average annual increase of more than 1 per cent between 1940 and 1960. Six of these fifteen counties enjoyed an average annual increase of more than 2 per cent.

Rates of increase varied from a low of 2 per cent in Limestone County to a high of 121 per cent in Mobile County. The figure for Mobile County represents an average annual increase during the twenty-year period of more than 6 per cent.

The ten largest counties in 1960 held 53 per cent of the state's population. These same counties held only 40 per cent of the population in 1940.

In terms of absolute increase there were four counties whose population increased by more than 50,000 persons during the twenty-year period. Two of these, Jefferson and Mobile, increased by more than 170,000 persons. Increases of between 15,000 and 35,000 persons were experienced in five counties and increases of less than 15,000 in twelve counties. Four of these counties had increases of less than 3,500 persons.

The majority of counties in Alabama showed a net decrease in population between 1940 and 1960. In the forty-six counties with net decreases, the rate of decrease ranged from less than 1

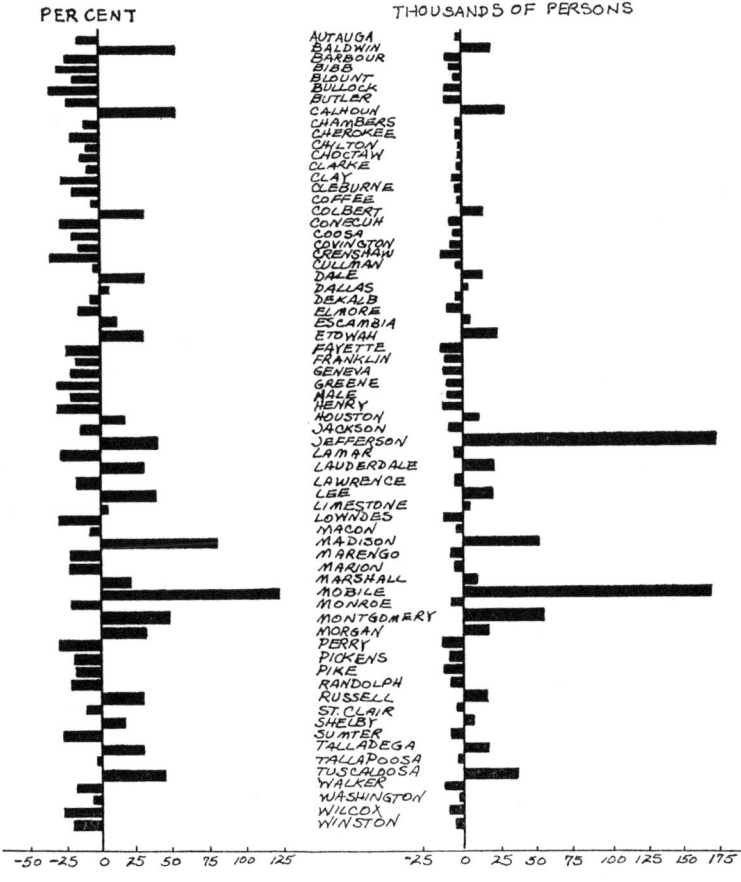

FIGURE 4

CHANGES IN POPULATION BY COUNTIES ALABAMA 1940 TO 1960

Source: U.S. Census of Population, 1950 and 1960, Alabama, Number of Inhabitants, PC(1)-2A.

per cent in Tallapoosa County to nearly 37 per cent in Crenshaw County. Twenty-six of these counties decreased in population by more than 20 per cent, and nine decreased by less than 10 per cent during the twenty years observed.

Despite the large number of counties with high rates of decrease in population, the relatively small size of these counties held the sum of decreases to 231,000 persons. In no county did the decrease amount to as many as 10,000 persons; the average (both mean and median) county decreases were between 5,000 and 6,000 persons.

The increase of population in a few large counties was almost three times the decrease in population experienced in the majority of Alabama's counties from 1940 to 1960, resulting in a net gain of 434,000.

HOUSEHOLDS

One would expect that as population changes there would be a correlative change in households. This has been true in Alabama; however, during the past twenty years households have increased at a rate nearly double that of population. In 1960 there were 884,000 households in the state, or nearly one-third more than the 675,000 households enumerated in the 1940 census. Population during the period increased only about one-sixth.

In 1940 there was an average of 4.2 persons per household. By 1960 this average had decreased to 3.6 persons per household. In three counties, Mobile, Dale, and Lowndes, the average number of persons per household increased between 1950 and 1960, going against the general trend for the state. There was substantial variation in 1960 in the average number of persons per household in the several Census-defined population areas. There was an average of 3.4 persons per household in urban areas (other than urban fringe) and in rural places of more than one thousand persons, 3.7 persons in urban fringe areas, and 3.9 persons in other rural areas.

Data for counties are not available for 1940. However, for

the state as a whole the more rapid increase of households relative to population change was slightly more pronounced between 1940 and 1950 than during the following decade.

NONWHITE AND NEGRO POPULATION

Alabama has a large nonwhite population of which the state's 980,000 Negroes represent more than 99 per cent. During the past twenty years the Negro population has remained practically constant, having decreased by less than one-half of 1 per cent in the 1940's and increased by less than one-tenth of 1 per cent in the 1950's. Despite the fact that during the past hundred years the number of Negroes in the population has increased in each decennial census, except 1920 and 1950, there has been since 1870 a rather steady decline in the ratio of Negroes to whites. Negroes numbered 475,000 and represented nearly 48 per cent of the population in 1870; in 1960 their number had more than doubled but they represented only 30 per cent of the population due to the more rapid increase in the white population.

Underneath these statistics there are more significant facts. Over the two decades, 1940 to 1960, the natural increase of nonwhites amounted to 38 per cent as compared with 37 per cent for the white population. Out-migration of Negroes, however, exceeded the natural increase by more than 3,000 persons; whereas out-migration of whites was substantially less than the natural increase. Thus, despite a higher birth rate, the nonwhite population decreased about one-tenth of 1 per cent against a 23 per cent increase for the white population between 1940 and 1960.

In 1950 there were fourteen counties in Alabama with Negro majorities; in 1960 there were only twelve. Negro majorities narrowed in ten of the counties and widened in two, Hale and Sumter. No county lost the white majority it had in 1950.

Nonwhites other than Negroes have increased nearly fourfold since 1940. In 1960 this segment of the population numbered 2,860 persons, representing less than one-tenth of 1 per cent of the people in Alabama.

The net change in nonwhite population during the twenty years was a decrease of some 700 persons.

AGE AND SEX CHARACTERISTICS

We pointed out above that the total population increased between 1940 and 1960. This was likewise true of most age groups when the population is classified by units of five years.

There was an increase of both white males and females for all age groups except those between fifteen and thirty years which decreased. Among the nonwhites there were decreases in those age groups falling between fifteen and forty-five years. In both decades there were decreases of Negro males and increases of Negro females. These decreases reflect vividly the effects of net out-migration and particularly that occurring among the nonwhites.

Throughout the period of our study there have been fewer males than females in Alabama and the trend has been toward greater imbalance. In 1940 there were 97.7 males for each one hundred females. This ratio declined to 95.0 in 1960. While there existed the same diminishing trend for both whites and nonwhites, the ratios for the two racial groups differ significantly. For the whites there were 100.5 males per hundred females in 1940 and 96.9 in 1960. For the nonwhites there were only 92.6 males per hundred females in 1940 and still fewer, 90.7, in 1960.

Contrary to the tendency toward a decreasing ratio of males to females in the general population were the rising ratios for persons under eighteen years of age in both racial groups.

Since 1940 the median age of Alabama's people has increased a little more than two years. The median age of twenty-six years in 1960 was three and one-half years lower than the median age for the population of the United States, which increased only one-half year during the twenty-year period.

The median age of the white population in Alabama increased nearly four years and was somewhat over twenty-eight

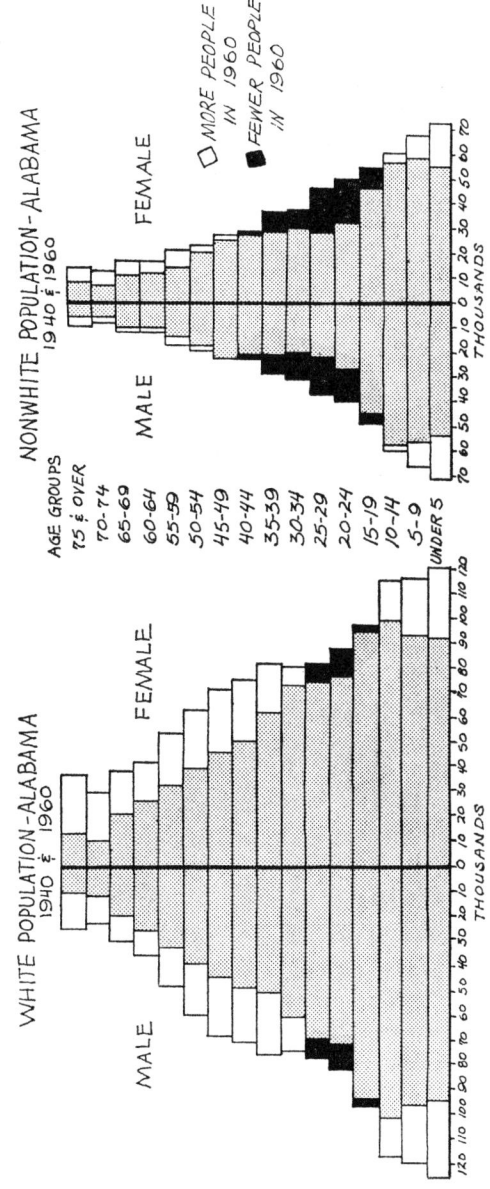

years in 1960, only two years lower than that of the white population of the United States, which had increased less than one year. The nonwhite median age, on the other hand, decreased by nearly two and one-half years and was a little more than twenty years in 1960. Alabama's nonwhite residents in 1960 averaged about three years younger than the nation's nonwhite population, whose median age had decreased only one and one-half years during the two decades.

Personal Income

THE BEST WAY TO COMPREHEND THE GREAT IMPROVEMENT IN personal income and consequently in the standard of living and in the consumer market in Alabama is to look at the dollar totals. The residents of Alabama had $800,000,000 to spend or save in 1940 and $4,800,000,000 in 1960. We wish to impress you, our readers, with the fact that this is a very great sum of money. Furthermore, while this five-fold increase in total personal income was occurring, the number of people among whom it was being distributed increased only 15 per cent.

The total personal income in our state increased every year of the twenty years between 1940 and 1960 except 1949 and 1954. It is a bigger sum, this total personal income, in Alabama than in any one of half of the conterminous 48 states. In other words, the Alabama consumer market is in the top half of state consumer markets.

The rate of growth of this big sum, over 500 per cent in twenty years, is as impressive as its bulk. Gross totals have definite and distinct worth in themselves, but let us now proceed to more refined, more scientific tests.

FIGURE 6
PER CAPITA PERSONAL INCOME-ALABAMA 1940, 1950 & 1960

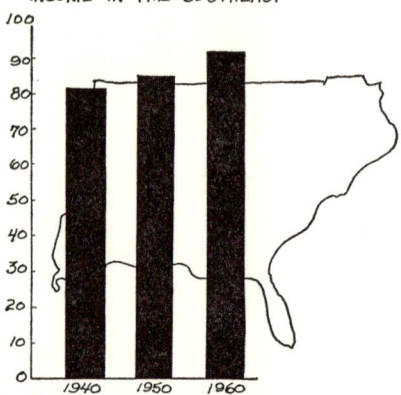

AS A PERCENTAGE OF PER CAPITA PERSONAL INCOME IN THE SOUTHEAST

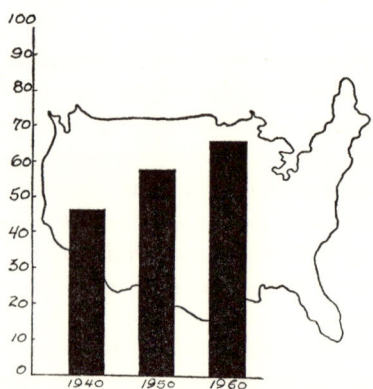

AS A PERCENTAGE OF PER CAPITA PERSONAL INCOME IN THE UNITED STATES

Sources: Personal Income by States Since 1929, a supplement to the Survey of Current Business, 1956; Survey of Current Business, April, 1961.

PERSONAL INCOME

Per capita personal income is the most used measurement. Alabama has always been low in per capita income among the other American states. In 1940 it had only $282 of personal income for each resident. This figure had risen to $1,462 by 1960. What each Alabamian had to spend advanced from 47 per cent of the national average to 66 per cent—or from less than half of the national average personal purchasing power to nearly two-thirds.

Still another way of portraying the rise in income in Alabama—and a way we like—is the pie. Yes, let's conceive of the annual personal income of the people of the whole nation as a huge lemon pie, round, thick, baked fresh yearly, with golden brown meringue on top. It gets bigger every year, too. Deeper, bigger around, every single year since 1939 except for a small loss in 1949.

The operations of the national and international market, more or less influenced by our government and foreign governments, slice the pie every year. Alabama's slice has been getting bigger—irregularly, but definitely (Figure 7). It is a wider slice of a larger pie that is coming to us.

At the same time that our share of the income is growing larger, our share of the population is growing smaller. In 1940 Alabama had 2.15 per cent of the nation's people, in 1950, 2.03 per cent, and in 1960, 1.83 per cent. With a growing share of the pie and a lessening proportion of the eaters, we live better and better.

In regard to disposable income Alabama does a little better than in total personal or per capita income. Disposable income is personal income less tax and nontax payments to government. In 1959 Alabama's per cent of conterminous United States total personal income was 1.21, of disposable income, 1.22.

Says the Office of Business Economics in the August, 1960, *Survey of Current Business,* page 13, in regard to the flow of disposable income, "These figures represent the best measure of consumer purchasing power available on a geographic basis. They are intended primarily for use by market analysts and

FIGURE 7
ALABAMA'S PERSONAL INCOME 6½ TIMES AS MUCH AS IT WAS TWENTY YEARS AGO

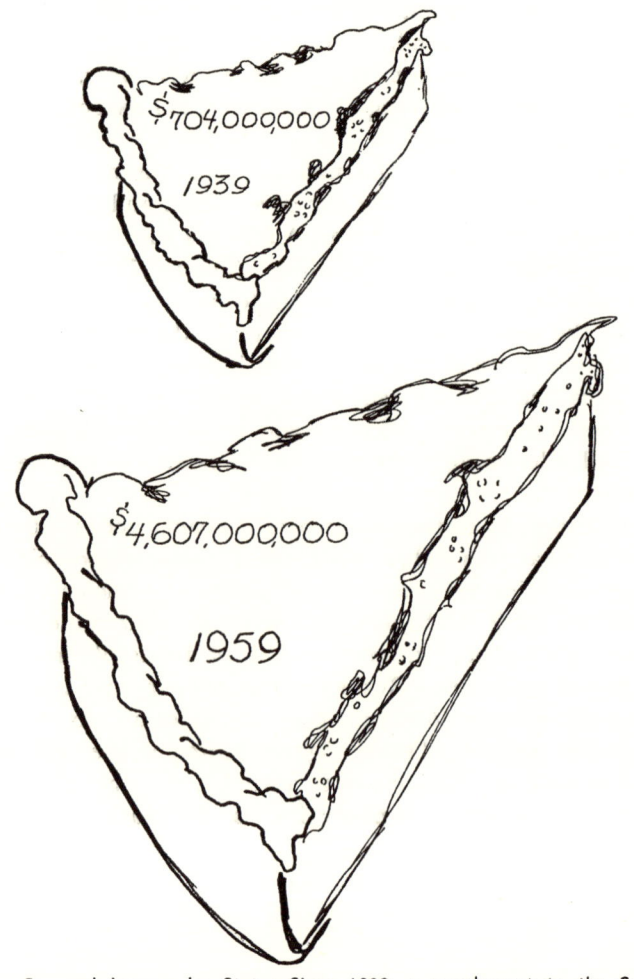

Sources: Personal Income by States Since 1929, a supplement to the Survey of Current Business, 1956; Survey of Current Business, August, 1960.

PERSONAL INCOME

others concerned with the actual dollar volume of consumer purchasing power in the various geographic markets."

Information on personal income by counties is available in Alabama. The Bureau of Business Research of the University of Alabama has published county income data back to 1939. The latest estimates appear annually in the May 15 issue of *Alabama Business*. It is available from the Bureau on request. It is so easy to get that is does not seem needful to draw from it extensively in this volume.

The leading ten counties enjoyed 65 per cent of the total personal income in 1959. Income increased in fifty-four of the sixty-seven counties from 1958 to 1959. It seems rather surprising that increasing income should occur in a substantial number of counties in which population is at present declining. New and better ways of making a living obviously must account for this fact.

Savings

CHANGES DURING THE PAST TWO DECADES HAVE BEEN AS FAR REACHing in the field of finance as anywhere in the economy of Alabama. The people have more money, they are saving more of it, they are borrowing and lending more of it. They are developing more skill in the management of money. More of them are making a living out of the management of money. Most important of all, they are becoming more thrifty.

All financial institutions in the old Confederate States were destroyed by the War. The return of security was delayed a decade by "Reconstruction." The National Bank System drew the money out of the South. The Federal Reserve System was much more equitable, but the financial pattern had been set by the time it was formed. And the South was not an area given to saving its money.

Banks were small and weak. Nowhere was all of this more true than in Alabama. It became necessary to look outside the state for financing. For a long time after the War the cotton crop was the biggest single source of a livelihood, and the main way of financing it was by borrowing on it before it was planted.

SAVINGS

Even as late as the beginning of the period we are studying, roughly two decades ago, advances by the planters to their tenants, loans by the "advancing merchants" to the farmers and by the bankers to the merchants, the planters and the farmers were important features of the economy. All were still often backed by crop liens. The publications of the Alabama Business Research Council have told a good part of the story of how the abandonment of these practices came about.

Everywhere the new ways of making a living brought more money. That was why people took to them. With the new money came more, larger, more diversified and more specialized financial institutions.

The commercial banks felt the economic changes and took part in making them. As the public deposited more money in the banks, making available more funds for loans, the bankers increased their loan deposits. They made their enlarged loans with skill and success. Total resources of commercial banks grew faster in Alabama than in the country as a whole. Resources of the nation's banks grew three-fold between 1940 and 1960. In the same period the resources of Alabama's banks gained four-and-one-half-fold. They now amount to four-fifths of one per cent of the national total (Table 4).

The national banks held more than two-thirds of the resources in commercial banking institutions in Alabama between 1940 and 1960. Time deposits in commercial banks in Alabama amounted to about 40 per cent of demand deposits in both 1940 and 1960, but were relatively much lower in 1950.

Life insurance was the second financial institution to become of importance in Alabama. It took the lead in teaching thrift. By 1940 the interest of Alabamians in providing for their dependents had made life insurance important in the economy of the state. The amount of life insurance written in 1940 was $216,000,000, life insurance premiums received were $28,000,000, and life insurance in force amounted to $1,046,000,000. Since then its growth has been steady. From 1940 to 1959, the amount of life insurance written annually increased nearly eight-fold.

The total premiums received annually grew six-fold. The total amount of insurance in force gained seven-fold.

By 1960 the total amount of life insurance in force in the state had reached nearly eight and a quarter billions. In 1958 with less than six and three-quarter billions, Alabama ranked twenty-third among the states in volume of life insurance in force. In 1960 Alabama's rank among the states was twenty-second. It had 1.4 per cent of the insurance in force in the country. The sales made in Alabama in 1960 were 1.7 per cent of those made in the nation, and the average amount owned per Alabama family was $8,500. Firms chartered in northern states started the life insurance business in Alabama, and it was not until the first decade of this century that a good start was made

TABLE 4. SELECTED STATISTICS OF COMMERCIAL BANKS, ALABAMA AND THE UNITED STATES
1940, 1950, AND 1960
(thousands of dollars)

	1940	1950	1960	Per cent change	
				1940 to 1950	1950 to 1960
Total assets:					
United States	70,710,864	166,552,184	289,750,147	+136	+ 74
Alabama	425,538	1,374,968	2,350,272	+223	+ 71
Per cent of					
United States	.60	.82	.81		
Demand deposits:					
United States	47,712,672	116,896,796	154,892,149	+145	+ 33
Alabama	268,120	1,013,786	1,507,053	+278	+ 49
Per cent of					
United States	.56	.87	.97		
Time deposits:					
United States	15,748,744	36,391,669	72,582,677	+131	+ 99
Alabama	107,324	257,526	613,666	+140	+138
Per cent of					
United States	.68	.71	.85		

Source: Federal Deposit Insurance Corporation.

SAVINGS 39

in Alabama by home life insurance companies. By 1940 the domestic companies were firmly established but still far behind the companies of other states.

TABLE 5. LIFE INSURANCE IN FORCE IN ALABAMA
(millions of dollars)

1940	1,046
1950	2,851
1960	8,231

Source: Institute of Life Insurance, New York.

During the two decades which comprise the period of our study, all life insurance did well, and the Alabama companies made gains that are astonishing. In 1940 the Alabama companies wrote about a fifth as much insurance as the out-of-state companies, collected an eighth the volume of premiums, and had a seventh as much insurance in force. By 1959 the Alabama companies wrote 58 per cent as much as the out-of-state companies, collected premiums equal in amount to 40 per cent of theirs, and had a volume of insurance in force equal to 40 per cent of theirs.

As of January 1961, there were 43 life insurance companies incorporated in Alabama. They had over half a billion dollars in assets and more than five billions of insurance in force. Both assets and insurance in force have more than doubled since 1954.

So far we have been speaking of all forms of life insurance combined. Now a little about the different kinds. Ordinary life amounted to nearly half of the total. Alabama sales of ordinary in 1960 were more than twice as large as those made here five years earlier. Group insurance comes next in volume, industrial is third, with credit the lowest in volume among the four big divisions of insurance.

Benefit payments are the reason for the existence of life insurance. In Alabama living and death benefits amounted to more than $83,000,000 during 1960. This is about double the amount it was eight years ago. In addition to these vast sums, over $32,000,000 were paid by life insurance companies to holders of hospital, surgical, medical, and loss-of-income policies.

Sharing of risk is the prime purpose of life and health insurance. But there are added benefits. Insurance is a business and a good one. Insurance is a medium of capital formation. It not only forms capital but is a source of financing for individuals, corporations, and governments. The nation's life insurance companies had three-quarters of a billion dollars invested in mortgages in Alabama in 1960. They also owned more than one hundred million dollars worth of Alabama state and municipal bonds.

The figures for some very important savings media (stocks, bonds, and other securities) cannot be broken down by states. No estimates of the amounts of any types of securities held in Alabama will be attempted.

But there are four more kinds of financial institutions, primarily savings media, on which there are reliable statistics. One of these four, the mutual savings banks, are not represented in Alabama. The other three are the savings and loan associations, the credit unions, and the postal savings system.

Of the three, savings and loan associations have far the largest amount of savings and are a close second to the commercial banks in the size of their holdings. The savings and loan associations are growing very rapidly. Savings deposited in these institutions increased nearly six-fold in the last decade alone, rising steadily to a total of $423,000,000 at the end of 1960. Alabama then ranked thirty-first among the states in the amount of savings in these associations as well as in all savings media combined.

A comparison of postal savings with credit unions is very thought-provoking. The postal savings system was started when popular confidence in private financial institutions was at a rather low point. It was thought that there were many people whose deposits only the Federal Government could bring in. In 1960 this savings medium accounted for only a little over $9,000,000.

SAVINGS

TABLE 6. SAVINGS IN SAVINGS AND LOAN ASSOCIATIONS, CREDIT UNIONS, AND POSTAL SAVINGS, ALABAMA
(millions of dollars)

Year	Savings and loan associations	Credit unions	Postal savings
1939	11.2	1.2	9.3
1945	23.9	3.5	28.4
1950	61.3	8.3	31.7
1955	179.4	27.3	23.4
1960	423.0	71.5	9.2

Sources: United States Savings and Loan League; Federal Home Loan Bank Board; Credit Union National Association; U. S. Bureau of Labor Statistics; House Documents No. 537, 76th Congress, and No. 399, 82nd Congress.

Credit unions did not appear in the statistics until twenty-five years ago. They attest the willingness of working people to keep and manage their own money. They are the farthest extreme from postal savings. From the most recent statistics, it appears that the resources of credit unions in Alabama amount to more than six times the postal savings. This is evidence that the self-reliance of the average man is greater than he is usually given credit for.

The growth in all of these financial institutions is bringing Alabama into a far better position to provide for its capital needs out of its own funds. Charles Taylor, an economist with the Federal Reserve Bank of Atlanta, has summed up the process that is going on in this way:

> . . . the future of the Southern economy is tied closely to that of the nation. If we assume that this nation's economic growth will continue, we may also conclude, on the basis of experience, that the South will continue to increase its share of expanding income. Under these conditions, consumer spending will continue to grow somewhat more rapidly in this area than elsewhere.
>
> As incomes increase, however, and the average income in the South more closely approaches that in the nation, the

strength of factors that brought about a tendency for Southerners to spend more of their incomes tends to diminish. As his income has increased, the Southern consumer has become more like the average American consumer. He saves more and spends less. Indeed, this has been going on ever since the South began to catch up in income.[1]

[1] Federal Reserve Bank of Atlanta, *Monthly Review*, Sept., 1960, p. 4.

Housing

THE HOUSES PEOPLE LIVE IN ARE REFLECTIONS OF THE STANDARD OF living that is being maintained. The standard of living in turn is a guide to the quality of the consumer market.

Both the number and quality of housing units in Alabama have increased during the past two decades. There were nearly 968,000 housing units in 1960, an increase of almost 37 per cent since 1940.

In defining a housing unit, the Census states that a group of rooms or a single room is regarded as a housing unit when it is occupied or intended for occupancy as separate living quarters.

Over 91 per cent of the housing units in Alabama were occupied in 1960. This was slightly higher than the occupancy figure for the nation. Of the 884,000 occupied housing units about 60 per cent were owner occupied. While this figure is a little less than the 62 per cent owner-occupied housing units for the United States, we find contrasting results when considering ownership by color. There are higher levels of ownership among whites and nonwhites in Alabama than among these groups in

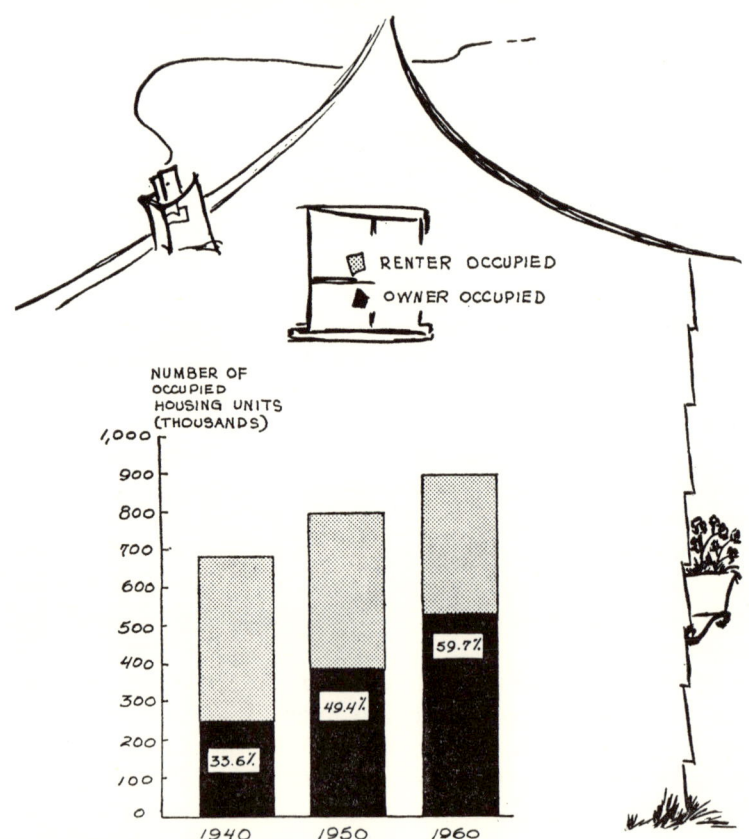

FIGURE 8

OWNER & RENTER OCCUPIED HOUSING UNITS, ALABAMA 1940, 1950 & 1960

Sources: U. S. Census of Housing, 1940, 1950, and Advance Reports, 1960, Housing Characteristics, States, Alabama, HC(A1)-1.

HOUSING

the nation. In Alabama 66 per cent of white housing units and 42 per cent of nonwhite housing units are owner occupied. Comparable figures for the United States are 64 per cent and 38 per cent, respectively. In addition to the occupied housing units nearly 35,000 vacant units, about 3.6 per cent of all units, were available for sale or rent. This was about 6 per cent higher than the United States ratio of 3.4 per cent.

During the past two decades, owner-occupied housing units have more than doubled while renter-occupied units declined one-fifth. White owner-occupied housing units increased 141 per cent as compared to a 104 per cent increase in non-white owner-occupied housing units. While both white and nonwhite renter-occupied housing units declined, the 29 per cent decrease for nonwhites was more than double the 14 per cent decrease for whites.

Sixty-seven per cent of the housing units in which people were living were said to be sound.[1] Another 22 per cent were considered to be deteriorating, and 12 per cent were dilapidated. This represents the achievement since 1950 of a 52 per cent reduction in the proportion of occupied housing units considered to be unfit for shelter.

Not only has there been an improvement in the state of repair of housing units in Alabama but also there has been an additional improvement in the standard of living they provide. This is indicated by changes which have taken place in plumbing facilities. In 1960 persons living in 61 per cent of the housing units could boast of having full plumbing facilities. Ten years earlier only those persons living in 32 per cent of occupied units could make such claim.

---

[1] The 1960 Census classified the condition of housing units according to whether they were "sound," "deteriorating," or "dilapidated." The Census defines sound housing as that which has no defects, or only slight defects which are normally corrected during the course of regular maintenance. Deteriorating housing needs more repair than would be provided in the course of regular maintenance. Dilapidated housing does not provide safe and adequate shelter.

FIGURE 9

CHANGE IN CONDITION OF OCCUPIED HOUSING UNITS --- ALABAMA 1940, 1950 & 1960

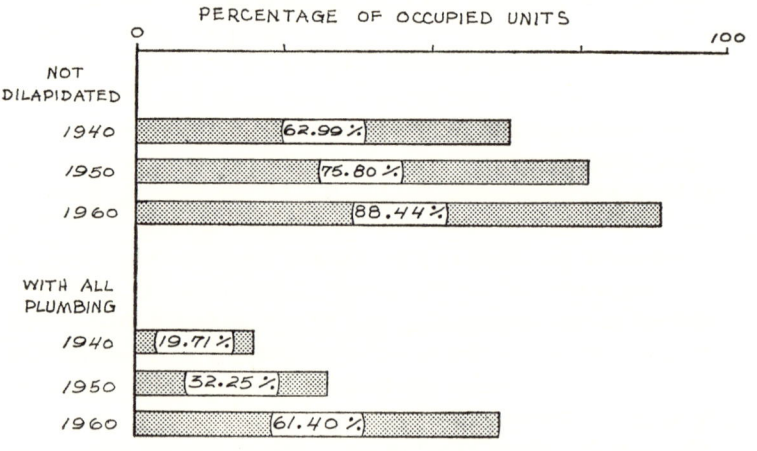

Sources: U. S. Census of Housing, 1940, 1950, and Advance Reports, 1960, Housing Characteristics, States, Alabama, HC(A1)-1.

HOUSING

That dramatic changes have occurred is further indicated by considering plumbing facilities in 1940. Then only 34 per cent of dwelling units reported running water inside the dwelling unit. Twenty-nine per cent reported use of inside flush toilet and 24 per cent reported bathtub or shower in the structure.

But this was twenty years ago. Since then vast improvements have been made in the houses Alabama's people live in.

Today the highest standard of housing accommodations is found among housing units occupied by white owners. Seventy-three per cent of the housing units in this group are sound, and have all plumbing facilities. By contrast, only 14 per cent of the housing units occupied by nonwhite renters are both sound and have all plumbing facilities.

It is important to note that the largest increase in housing units has been in the group occupied by white owners and the largest decrease in the group occupied by nonwhite renters.

These changes, pointing to better housing for the people of Alabama, are closely related to the movement of population from rural to urban areas and the widespread introduction of electric power throughout the state. These two factors stimulate rising demand in virtually every area of consumption to accompany the rising quality of housing.

PART II: GREEN HILLS AND VALLEYS

Agricultural Transformation

FARMING IS NOT A POPULAR OCCUPATION IN ALABAMA. MANY MORE people are leaving it than are entering it. This has been true during the last two decades, is still true today.

During 1958 the Alabama Business Research Council published a detailed study of Alabama agriculture in a changing economy. The report bears one of those rare titles that serve both as a heading and as a summary: *Flight From the Soil.*

The Research Committee made use of the 1954 *Census of Agriculture* and earlier ones and some annual figures available for the years 1955 and 1956. Facts and conclusions drawn from these sources were rather fully presented. In addition, a major contribution to the study of American farms and farm life was made in Part II of the report, entitled "The Case." Members of the Research Committee questionnaired more than 700 employees of their own firms who had come from the farm. The questionnaires contain an adequate description of the backgrounds of these refugees from the soil, of their reasons for quitting farming, and of the conditions under which they might return. A variety of reasons, statistical and otherwise, lead us to believe that the attitudes revealed in this case study are still prevalent.

The 1958 study was so thorough and is so readily available that it seems necessary for us only to bring up to date the items that bear on the farm sector of the economy.

Flight from the soil continued at an accelerating pace. In the five years between the agricultural censuses of 1954 and 1959, the number of farms in Alabama fell from 176,956 to 115,610. Fourteen thousand of these dropouts are accounted for by a change in the Census definition of the word farm. At least one farmer in four in Alabama quit the farm between 1954 and 1959. The average size of farm continued to grow with the decline in number of farms. The average number of acres in an Alabama farm was 76.4 in 1920, 117.6 in 1954, and 143.0 in 1959. The national average is 320.0 acres per farm, so Alabama farms are still relatively small.

The farms in 1959 would have been still bigger but for a noteworthy drop in the percentage of the state's land area in farms. This figure fell from 63.7 per cent in 1954 to only 50.6 per cent in 1959. This is almost identical with the 1925 figure, 51.0 per cent. So the proportion of the state's area included in farms had grown slowly over a generation from half to nearly two-thirds, then dropped back in only five years to where it had been 34 years earlier. That is the most marked reversal of trend—indeed the only notable reversal of trend—occurring between the picture presented in *Flight From the Soil* and that shown by the 1959 *Census of Agriculture*.

One feature of Alabama farming that has shown no recent trend at all is the color of the farmers. About three-fourths (74 per cent) were white both in 1954 and 1959. It will be very interesting to observe whether a trend develops in the next few years.

But while the faces of the farmers do not change, the face of the soil is changing fast. Crops are lessening in importance, pasture and forestry are gaining. Less than 30,000 of the 115,000 farms are classed as cotton farms. There are 16,000 livestock

FIGURE 10

PERCENTAGE OF LAND IN FARMS ALABAMA 1920 TO 1959

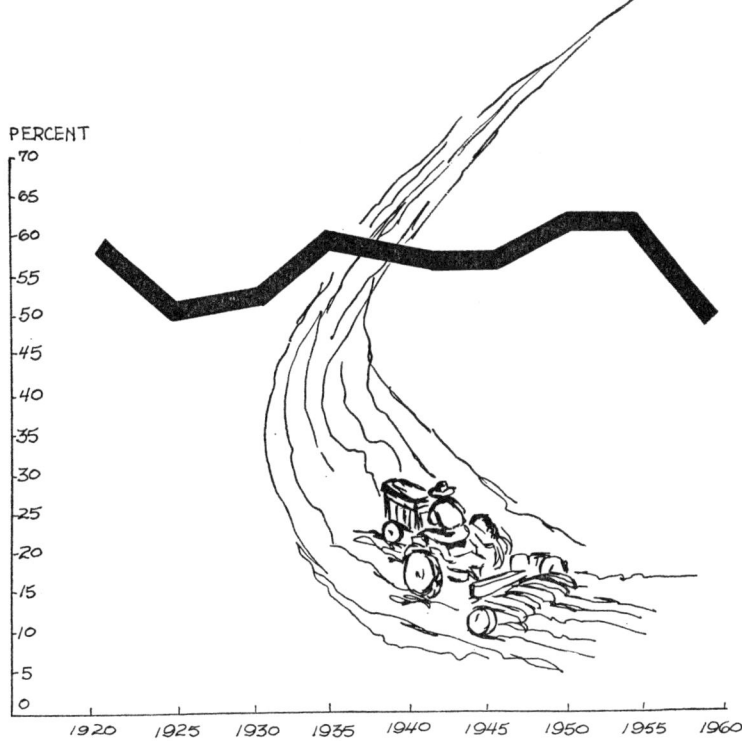

Sources: U. S. Census of Agriculture, 1954 and 1959 (AC 59-1, preliminary).

farms, including dairy and poultry. There are more and more specialized farms, with specialized equipment.

Even cotton is no longer, by any means, a hand-cultivated crop. Machines are extensively used and chemicals are gaining rapidly. To give the reasons why, we quote from *Farm Journal,* April, 1961, page 41:

> "Two reasons [for use of chemicals to control grass and weeds]," answers Lamar Lowe of Cherokee County, Ala., who treated his 60 acres last year: "First, it cuts your hoe bill at least in half; and second, we can't get hoe labor even if we could afford it."
>
> Some 21% of the cotton acreage in Cherokee County was pre-emergence treated last year, reports county agent J. J. Young. "When farmers didn't have equipment, they swapped work or hired it done."
>
> Millard Lecroy, for example, used pre-emergence chemicals on his 60 acres in 1960, then planted 200 acres for neighbors who furnished the seed and Karmex DL.

It takes more money now than ever before to be a farmer. The average value of land and buildings went up from $6,223 in 1954 to $11,822 in 1959. When we add in the needed equipment and working capital, we can see why in some lines of farming it takes as much capital per worker to operate as it does in some manufacturing.

We are not speaking here of part-time farmers with little patches of ground, but of the real farmers who make their main living out of farming. It is customary now, not only for the Bureau of the Census but for all students of agriculture, to call these people "commercial farmers."

The commercial farmers produce most of the farm products of all kinds. There are not very many of them, only 33,528, whose sales come to more than $2,500 a year. Another 24,217 get most of their living from farming, but sell less than $2,500 of products a year. The Census calls them commercial farmers, Class VI. The Alabama Business Research Council, in *Flight From the Soil,* aptly terms those with incomes of less than $1,200, "mar-

AGRICULTURAL TRANSFORMATION

ginal farmers." In view of the 1961 standard of living in Alabama, we shall call all of the commercial farmers who make less than $2,500 a year from farming "marginal." We think they will continue to be drawn away from farming into other occupations. The other 57,000—half of all farmers—are part-time farmers. They live on farms but not off of them, primarily at least.

TABLE 7. CASH RECEIPTS FROM FARM MARKETINGS, ALABAMA
(millions of dollars)

1939	87,000
1944	277,000
1949	351,200
1950	361,400
1951	447,900
1952	452,900
1953	438,000
1954	400,300
1955	471,000
1956	465,800
1957	412,200
1958	486,800
1959	518,841
1960	532,598

Sources: 1939 and 1944, Statistical Bulletin No. 246, March, 1959, USDA; 1949 to 1958, *The Farm Income Situation*, FIS-179 (supp.), August, 1960, USDA; 1959 and 1960, *The Farm Income Situation*, FIS-183, July, 1961, USDA.

Flight From the Soil commented on the changes in components of cash receipts from farm marketings. Cotton has dropped from an average of 72.8 per cent of the total in 1925-29 to 27.3 per cent in 1955-59. In 1960 cotton provided less than a fourth (24 per cent) of the cash receipts from farm marketings in Alabama. Livestock and products meantime had come up from an average of 15.2 per cent of all farm products in 1925-29 to 51.1 in 1955-59. In 1960 the figure was 56.7. Figures for 1960 are: livestock and products marketings, $302,062,000, and crop marketings, $230,536,000.

The most spectacular recent change in Alabama agriculture is the swift drop in farm tenancy. Nearly half the farm tenants in Alabama disappeared between the farm censuses of 1954 and 1959. At the latter date, there were only 32,228 left. This trend cannot continue at the same pace because, if it did, the state would run out of tenants before the end of 1965. This change is as tremendous in its social as in its economic implications. Alabama's farmers are now landowners, with all that this implies.

Attention was called in *Flight From the Soil* to the fact that in recent years Alabama ranked among the lowest states in net income per farm and that its net income per farm was less than one-half the average for the United States. In 1960 this had ceased to be true; average net income per farm in Alabama had advanced to $1,597, compared with $2,568 for the nation. Alabama's average net farm income exceeded those of Kentucky, Louisiana, Mississippi, South Carolina, Tennessee, Vermont, Virginia, and West Virginia.

From a business viewpoint, the gross income of the farmers is more important than the net. What the farmer has for his personal consumption comes from net income, but his operating expenditures as a farmer are a function of his gross income. This is, of course, much larger than the net. The average Alabama farmer in 1960 grossed $4,051. However, this was less than half the national gross of $8,362. Gross farm incomes were smaller in only five states: Kentucky, Mississippi, South Carolina, Tennessee, and West Virginia.

With *Flight From the Soil* reviewed and its statistical content brought up to date in the previous section, we are ready to attempt an appraisal of the farm market in Alabama. The first fact to remember is that the farm is an important market in this state, but not one of its biggest. We should bear in mind that only 5.8 per cent of the income of our people comes from farming. But it is equally important to bear in mind that the farm market here is an improved and still improving one. There are only two-thirds as many farmers to reach with advertising and selling efforts as there were just five years ago. Yet the market potential is much bigger. Gross farm income in Alabama for the five years 1955 to 1959, averaged $569,000,000 as compared with averages of $540,000,000 for 1950 to 1954, $480,000,000 for 1945 to 1949, and $275,000,000 for 1940 to 1944. A new high was reached in 1960 when gross farm income amounted to $634,000,000.

It is a better market, also, because approximately three out of four (71.7 per cent) of the farmers in 1959 were landowners. Alert sales managers are concerned with this change. The pride of ownership and the incentives for working harder that it supplies are vital conditions of the market. Farm credit is greatly strengthened by it. In the same five years that owner-operated farms have risen from two-thirds to nearly three-fourths of all farms, the size has risen sharply and the average value nearly doubled. The impact of these developments on the farmer's purchasing power and credit potential has been very heavy.

The sales manager who is working in the Alabama farm market must keep in the forefront of his mind that this is no longer a cotton state, but overwhelmingly a livestock state. Feed, feed supplements, growth hormones, and sanitation supplies stand out increasingly in sales to farmers. Pasture building is of greater concern than tillage. In the background, the growth of trees looms ever larger in importance.

The dealers in chain saws and wood hauling equipment have assumed a position similar to that ginners have had in Alabama. Sales of forest products are spreading widely and moving slowly but steadily upward. The farmer's woodland, in many instances, has taken the place of his traditional cotton patch.

Remember that the trees are treated now as a crop. Not only are trees planted in increasing number, but all the trees are cared for better. They are protected from fire and from depredations by animals. Indeed, when we ride over the state of Alabama now, we realize that Alabama is not going back to the Indians, but a great deal of it really is going back to the forest and to pastures.

Forestry in the New Economy

THE STORY OF THE FORESTS CANNOT REALLY BE TOLD SEPARATELY. IT is inextricably involved with the lumber manufacturing industry and with agriculture. But forestry is important enough to deserve a chapter of its own in this volume, and we give it one. The trees will serve as the central theme and will give unity to the narrative.

When the first English-speaking settlers came to Alabama, the trees were mostly obstacles to cultivating the soil. But some of the pioneers also saw the forests as free range for the livestock and places to hunt and take game and furs. When towns and transportation arose, a market for lumber developed and grew larger with the decades. Water-sawn lumber supplanted or at least supplemented hewn timber. As late as the second quarter of this century, it was still possible to find a surviving example, here and there, of the water-powered sawmill in production.

Steam was soon the dominant source of power and sawmills big and little were dotted over the whole state. About the turn of the century the big mill, with big landholdings and a railroad, dominated the scene. The virgin timber was about gone but the second growth was being cut. The "clean" cut was practiced. You did not hear of "selective cutting" until the last two or three decades.

The big mills had reforestation programs, but they cut out their big tracts before new growth was ready. They ran into trouble in the small tracts and many of them quit, went broke, or changed their methods of operation. A successful young lumberman at that time explained: "With the small tracts of saw timber that we have now, you can go into the woods with a little light portable mill and take the sawed boards to town or to the railroad for little or no more than it costs the big fellow to get his *logs* to his mill."

Everywhere in the state log railroads were abandoned. Many mills, too. However, some lumber operators, younger men usually, made huge fortunes, almost overnight, in the 1930's at that. One owned and operated 40 portable mills. Another said on his letterhead that he marketed for 104 mills. Each such operation had a concentration point where the lumber was measured, trimmed to exact size, put through a soda bath to keep the color fresh, and sorted for dimension and quality. Thus the small tracts were cut.

By the mid 1930's nearly all of the forests consisted of cutover woods, unpromising, and almost worthless. The end of lumbering as a big industry in Alabama seemed to many to be in sight.

In farming the picture was equally discouraging, and closely related. The chief connection was the habit of "farming with matches." This expression refers to the habit of the typical small farmer—owner or tenant—of going to the fields in the spring before plowing time with his bigger children and a box of matches. They set fire to every patch of dry grass, to every clump of weeds, to every stalk of corn or cotton. The land was made bare for easy plowing and planting. All sources of humus were destroyed. The soil leached poorer year by year. Experts once considered much of it beyond redemption. Farmers even burned their woodlands to make the grass come out better in the spring so that their livestock might pasture in the woods to better advantage.

The forests, too, were burned off, as often as they would burn. In a dry fall it was an unpleasant experience to travel even a few miles through the country. Smoke filled the air, hurt the eyes and nose, made visibility poor and driving unsafe.

"Fence law" held through most of the state. That meant that the landowner had to put up and maintain a fence around his own land. If his neighbor's stock broke in, it was the fault of the landowner, not of the cow's owner. Every small farmer who had any stock expected it to pasture in his neighbor's woods—and along the highways. Among the chief hazards to driving were the cows and hogs loose on the roads. Especially was this true on smoky evenings. The loose stock was almost invariably scrub stock. Furthermore, between fires and dogs running wild, it seemed that wild game was on its way to extermination.

Wise men in all times and many places disapproved of these practices and spoke out against them. But they were usually ignored. Many leaders even openly approved. A prominent botanist said and wrote that fire was beneficial in the woods and probably played a leading part in the farming of the great primeval forests, especially the long leaf pine. This view still finds support.

There were natural allies in the fight for trees. The good row-crop farmers, the good stock farmers, the sawmill men, the timber landowners, the sportsmen, the more intelligent citizens in general could see the sense of conservation. It appears that the small farmers were won over by goodwill, patience, and neighborliness. The main things wanted of the small farmers were to get them to stop setting fire to the woods and fields, and to pen up their dogs.

A new factor in the forestry picture—the paper mill—had been on the horizon for some years. In the 1930's when it appeared that paper mills were to become important in the forestry industry, the pessimists predicted not only the end of the lumber business but the certain doom of our forests as well. The head timber consultant for a great railway system said, "This is the end of your conservation program; they take the small trees." It took some years to recognize how wrong he was.

This brief review of the forest situation in Alabama before 1940 is necessary in order to comprehend the developments since 1940. These have been rapid, as profound as any we have related.

In the story of the trees since 1940 the paper mills have probably played the largest and most dynamic part. There were nine pulp mills in the state in 1960 with a total daily capacity of 4,693 tons. Alabama is the second state in the union in pulpwood production.

Pulpwood harvesting is still partly on an extractive basis in Alabama. About 40 per cent of the round pulpwood—cord wood —is shipped out of the state. A fourth of the total goes to Florida and small amounts go to each of the other states that touch Alabama. Some of this is a mere matter of proximity to the mill. We import some wood, but only a little more than a fourth of the amount we export. Nearly all of the imported wood is from Mississippi. A tiny quantity does come from Florida, but none is received from the other contiguous states. Thus, despite its rapid growth over the past two decades, paper manufacturing in Alabama still does not utilize the state's current capacity for production of pulpwood. In this respect paper manufacturing is less advanced in Alabama than the predominant industries.

In conservation the paper industry is highly advanced. About the middle of the forties machinery began to be installed in the lumber mills and other wood-using plants which converted much of the tree residue into paper mill chips. There were 141 of these installations operating in Alabama in 1960, and they furnished nearly one-seventh of the pulpwood.

The growing and cutting of pulpwood is an important factor in Alabama's expanding markets. It is produced in every county in the state. Its production is on the increase as is shown in Figure 11, which compares the production of pulpwood and lumber. In 1946 pulpwood production was only about one-fifth

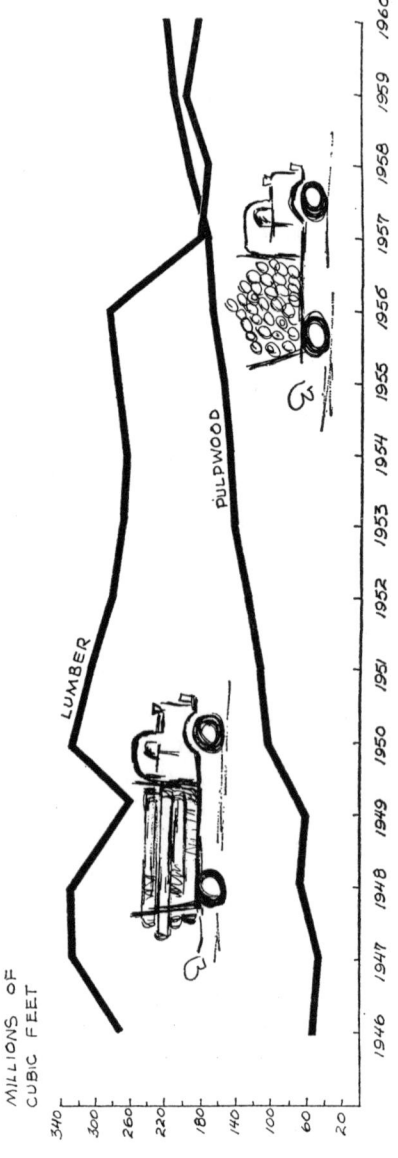

FIGURE 11

PRODUCTION OF LUMBER & PULPWOOD, ALABAMA
1946 TO 1960
(CUBIC FEET)

NOTE: LUMBER CONVERTED AT 156 CUBIC FEET PER 1,000 BOARD FEET
PULPWOOD CONVERTED AT 77 CUBIC FEET PER CORD

Sources: Annual Report, 1959/60, and "Production of Forest Products by Counties in Alabama—Calendar Year 1960," State of Alabama Department of Conservation.

FORESTRY IN THE NEW ECONOMY 61

as large as lumber production, but by 1960 it had grown to be nearly 20 per cent larger. Pulpwood production is not restricted to pine trees, as many think. About one-sixth of the total output in 1959 consisted of hardwood.

We shall not need to devote as much space to the other wood uses as to pulpwood. Table 8 presents the statistics in brief. Some economic analysis of the lumber manufacturing and pulp and paper industries is presented in the next chapter.

TABLE 8. AVERAGE PRODUCTION OF FOREST PRODUCTS, ALABAMA, 1958-60 COMPARED TO 1952-54

Product	Annual average 1952-54	Annual average 1958-60	Per cent change
Pine lumber, 1,000 board feet	1,077,330	765,162	—29.0
Hardwood lumber, 1,000 board feet	550,219	423,311	—23.1
Total lumber, 1,000 board feet	1,627,549	1,188,473	—27.0
Pulpwood, chemical wood, cords	1,540,800	1,811,533	+17.6
Crossties, switch ties, pieces	1,561,478	909,214	—41.8
Mine ties, pieces	165,831	55,707	—66.4
Mine props, pieces	2,196,240	655,020	—70.2
Crude turpentine, 400-lb. barrels	42,463	30,426	—28.3
Stumpwood, tons	250,594	315,716	+26.0
Poles and piling, pieces	475,141	385,821	—18.8

Sources: *Annual Report,* 1959/60, and "Production of Forest Products by Counties in Alabama—Calendar Year 1960," State of Alabama Department of Conservation.

The protection, reproduction, and improvement of trees is of vital importance to the perpetuation and advancement of this whole agricultural-industrial complex. A program to carry this out is already well developed in Alabama. It has the support of the local, state, and federal governments, of private enterprise, and, what is most important, of the general public.

Fire, disease, and crowding by weed trees are the chief enemies of the valuable tree. The deadliest of these, fire, is the one on which most effort is now expended. The State Department of Conservation administers the program, the timberland owners, the lumber and paper mill owners, and the United States Forest Service cooperate. The old "fence laws" or "stock laws" are gone, and effective legal protection against forest fires now exists. Public opinion is against burning the woods and both number and size of fires are lessening. Fire towers dot the land and the whole state is kept under constant watch.

The reforestation program is tremendous and growing. Fourteen times as many trees were planted in 1950-1959 as in the previous decade. It is estimated that at least 1,100,000 acres of land have been reforested in Alabama. Professional foresters are licensed in Alabama and their services are available in every county. The growth of the trees in this state is estimated at about one-third greater than the cut.

The Federal Government has established some large national forests in the state and the organized private forestry efforts have been still more extensive. The Tree Farm movement is national in scope and well developed in Alabama. This program is a private effort supported voluntarily by taxpaying owners of timberland. The Alabama laws do not assess the tree growth for taxation but impose a severance tax on the cut.

At the end of 1960 Alabama was the second state in the nation in both the number and acreage of tree farms.

Many benefits from the revolution in forestry besides those so far indicated in this sketch accrue to many people in this state. Some of these benefits are economic and some are not. Relief from the smoke of the great, unchecked fires is both a gain for comfort and for health. The green hills and valleys unscarred by fire have given Alabama a new look, pleasing to the eye. The increase in game population is a source of enjoyment to many.

But the heart of the matter is that the land is green.

PART III: INDUSTRY AND BASIC SERVICES

Farm Fields to Factory Sites

THE INDUSTRIAL ECONOMY OF ALABAMA CONTINUES TO EXPAND and to diversify. In the initial Alabama Business Research Council publication, *Alabama's Manufacturing Economy,* the opening paragraph states:

> Alabama is a rapidly industrializing area. The economic face of the state is changing, and by historic standards is changing with almost incredible speed. In less than two decades, factories stand in what used to be cotton fields, manufacturing industries hitherto unknown in Alabama have become commonplace, and virtually every community in the state has become an aggressive bidder for the location of new manufacturing establishments.

This report, published in 1955, is recommended to you because it presents an excellent analysis of the changes which occurred in industry and which had a vital part in developing Alabama's economy from 1939 to the early 1950's. The present report will bring out new characteristics of Alabama's industry which are making Alabama grow as a market. Industrial organizations form a market for goods, provide wages which give the people purchasing power, demand services from other people, and provide profits for dividends and industry growth. The changes occurring in industry must be clarified and evaluated in terms of what the contributions have been and will be in the future.

On an overall basis, industry has been growing in recent years, but not at the pell-mell rate of the early 1940's. Employment is increasing in manufacturing but not at as fast a rate as in some other segments of the economy. The types of industry are changing in importance as employment expands in some industries and contracts in others. The contribution to the production of the United States, as measured by value added by manufacture, is increasing. There is less concentration in a few industries and the growing industries are less dependent on Alabama's natural resources. Some industries continue to increase their heavy capital investments to provide new plants and to expand and update existing facilities, but others are moving slowly. Through these shifts and changes Alabama's industrial sector continues to progress.

The annual investment by manufacturing industries in Alabama for expansion and modernization of production facilities during the years 1951 through 1955 ranged between 1.05 per cent and 1.30 per cent of annual industrial capital expenditures in the United States. It rose dramatically to 2.00 per cent and 2.33 per cent in 1956 and 1957, then dropped in 1958 to 1.49 per cent of the United States total, still substantially above the earlier level.

Investment by manufacturing firms during these latter three years totaled $614,000,000. The primary metals group made the largest capital expenditures during this period.

Combined industrial employment—mining; contract construction; manufacturing; and transportation, communications, and public utilities—has increased from 223,000 in 1939 to 312,000 in 1949, and to 341,000 in 1959. Manufacturing has had the greatest increase. However, when compared to Alabama's total non-agricultural employment, employment in these four industry groups shows a declining percentage; from 55 per cent in 1939, to 52 per cent in 1949, and to 45 per cent in 1959. Contract construction is the only one of this group that has increased its share of Alabama's non-agricultural employment. Much of this change in the pattern of industrial employment is due to the modernizing process of using machines which are more automatic, to the changing demands of the various industries, and to the greater percentage expansion of other segments of the economy.

The World War II years saw great growth in the number of manufacturing establishments due to the large demand for products such as metals, cloth, and building materials. During the period from 1939 to 1947 the number of establishments and number of employees increased by more than 50 per cent, and the value added by manufacture[1] increased by over 250 per cent. A more complete discussion of this change may be found in *Alabama's Manufacturing Economy,* the 1955 study of the Alabama Business Research Council.

To further stimulate this progress the Alabama State Planning and Industrial Development Board, many utility and industrial companies, and many local groups have been actively seeking industries and have been assisting communities in evaluating their assets and in making brochures to be used in attracting industries.

During the period 1947 to 1958 the number of manufacturing establishments increased from 3,335 to 3,923, an increase of 588. However, it is important to note that 558 establishments came into existence between 1947 and 1954. Of these, 221 were lumber and wood products firms established to meet war-delayed con-

[1] According to the U. S. Bureau of the Census, value added by manufacture is calculated by "substracting the cost of materials, supplies and containers, fuel, purchased electric energy, and contract work from the value of shipments for products manufactured plus receipts for services rendered." This difference, which is called "value added by manufacture," is made up of such items as direct and indirect labor cost, salaries, depreciation, interest cost, administrative expenses, advertising, overhead, and profit, if any.

sumer demand and Korean War need for wood products. Between 1954 and 1958 more than 250 lumber establishments went out of business and were replaced by other types of establishments such as machinery; printing; chemicals; fabricated metals; stone, clay, and glass; and furniture and fixtures. At the same time 30 more establishments were added. These industries improved Alabama's economy by expanding and diversifying the potential industrial market as will be indicated on the following pages.

The number of manufacturing establishments in Alabama increased nearly 18 per cent from 1947 to 1958. This increase was in the establishments with under 20 employees and in those with over 99 employees. Although the number of establishments with over 20 employees was exactly the same in 1947 and in 1958, there has been a shift upward in the size of employment among these plants. The group employing 100 or more people has grown by 80 establishments at the expense of the group employing 20 to 99 people.

During these years, as is shown in Figure 12, manufacturing employment has increased almost 24,000 people, a 12 per cent increase, and has concurrently shifted among industry groups. Employment in textiles dropped from roughly 52,000 in 1947 to 40,000 in 1958 while employment in the apparel industry increased from 8,000 to 22,000. Employment in lumber dropped 5,000 from 1954 to 1958 and in primary metals 4,000 from 1947 to 1958; although, as we shall see later, value added by manufacture in primary metals increased during this period.

Three industry groups, primary metals, textiles, and lumber, dominated manufacturing employment for many years, accounting for over 60 per cent of the state's manufacturing employment as late as 1947. By 1954 this had dropped to 52 per cent and by 1958 to 44 per cent of the total.

The net increase of 12 per cent in total employment, 1947 to 1958, is the result of rapid growth in other industries. Employment grew at various rates in the following industry groups: apparel, 174 per cent; transportation equipment, 117 per cent;

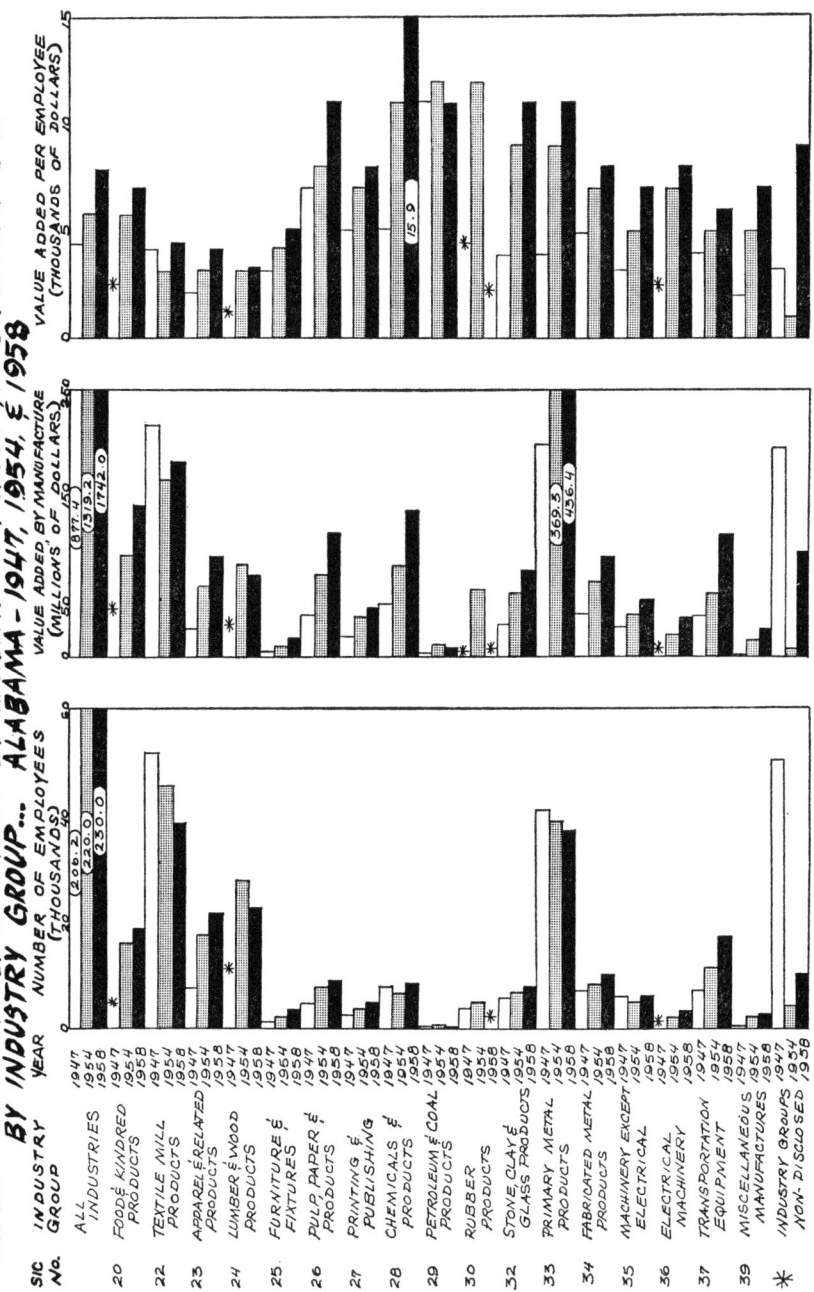

FIGURE 12

NUMBER OF EMPLOYEES, VALUE ADDED BY MANUFACTURE & VALUE ADDED PER EMPLOYEE BY INDUSTRY GROUP — ALABAMA — 1947, 1954, & 1958

Sources: U. S. Census of Manufactures, 1947, 1954, and 1958 (MC(P)-5, preliminary).

paper, 75 per cent; fabricated metals, 44 per cent; printing, 39 per cent; and stone, clay, and glass, 32 per cent. The effect of these changes has been to increase employment in establishments producing non-durable goods and to decrease employment in those producing durable goods.

Although primary metals and textiles remain the largest two employers in manufacturing, the industrial economy of Alabama has experienced marked diversification, especially in the past decade, and has thus become far less dependent on a few industries.

Along with diversification there has been a trend in Alabama toward the higher-wage industries. The fabricated metals, the transportation equipment, the paper, the printing, the chemical, the rubber products, and the petroleum industries are among the high-wage industries in Alabama which have had substantial increases in their employment. These six industry groups with average hourly earnings in 1958 ranging from $2.08 to $2.42 are valuable assets to the economy. Another valuable asset is the primary metals industry, the second largest in employment, which led with average hourly earnings of $2.61 in 1958.

The garment industry, with average hourly earnings of $1.19 in 1958, has expanded its employment very rapidly to fourth place in the state. Much of the employment in this industry (approximately 80 per cent are women) represents supplementary income to the family. It is beneficial also to the extent that the people employed would otherwise have been employed at lower wages or not employed at all.

The major drop in employment, 1947 to 1958, has been in textiles and lumber. These industries had average hourly earnings of $1.37 and less than $1.00, respectively, in 1958.

The growth of Alabama's industrial economy is indicated by the changes in the value added by Alabama's manufacturing industries. From 1939 to 1958 Alabama's value added by manufacture grew from $246,000,000 to $1,742,000,000, a 600 per cent increase, compared with an increase of 480 per cent in the national figure. During these twenty years, Alabama increased its share of the total value added for the United States by nearly 25 per cent, from 1.00 per cent in 1939 to 1.24 per cent in 1958. From 1947 to 1954 part of this gain was lost (0.05), but in the following four years the state again increased its share (0.11) as the result of a greater drive to bring industry to Alabama.

These efforts to attract industry to Alabama increased the dispersion of industry over the state. In 1939 only eighteen of Alabama's sixty-seven counties contributed as much as one-half of 1 per cent of the state's total value added by manufacture, but by 1958 ten counties had been added to this group. As a result of this, the relative share of the total value added by the top three counties—Jefferson, Mobile, and Etowah—declined from 62 per cent in 1939 to 51 per cent in 1958.

While Alabama's share of the value added by manufacture has increased, its share of the United States' employment has remained almost constant. As a result, Alabama's value added per employee increased from 82 per cent of the United States average in 1947 to 86 per cent in 1958.

TABLE 9. PERCENTAGE DISTRIBUTION OF VALUE ADDED BY MANUFACTURE, SELECTED COUNTY GROUPINGS, ALABAMA, 1939, 1947, 1954, AND 1958

County	1939	1947	1954	1958
Jefferson County	42.92	31.41	36.51	33.24
Mobile County	9.09	10.41	9.34	10.60
Etowah County	9.61	7.84	7.71	7.68
Subtotal	61.62	49.66	53.56	51.52
Next 15 counties	21.51	31.58	31.57	32.55
Subtotal	83.13	81.24	85.13	84.07
Next 10 counties	3.43	5.71	4.45	6.07
Subtotal	86.56	86.95	89.58	90.14
Remaining 39 counties	13.44	13.05	10.42	9.86
Total	100.00	100.00	100.00	100.00

Source: *U. S. Census of Manufactures*, 1947, 1954, and *Area Reports*, 1958, Alabama, MC (P)-S1.

A rising value added per employee indicates, in general, increasing industrial mechanization, higher wages and profits, and greater expenditures for associated services. It is to industries with these high productivity characteristics that the economy looks for progress; it is here that the industrial market is developed and an important share of the consumer purchasing power is provided.

In value added, as in employment, three industry groups—primary metals, textiles, and lumber—historically contributed over 60 per cent of the value added by manufacture; but their share dropped to 47 per cent in 1954 and to 40 per cent in 1958. In the textiles and the lumber industries the amount of value added actually dropped; but the primary metals industry continued to expand its contribution by more than doubling its value added from 1947 to 1958, even though its employment had dropped slightly. The lessening dependence on a few industries further emphasizes the trend toward diversification in Alabama. In 1939 only four industry groups—primary metals, textiles, lumber, and food—accounted for 70 per cent of the value added by Alabama's manufacturing industries; whereas in 1958 it took seven industry groups to account for 70 per cent. These were primary metals, textiles, food, chemicals, paper, transportation equipment, and apparel.

These changes in the industrial complex point to changes in the demand for materials, supplies, plant, and equipment.

Many of Alabama's newer and more rapidly growing industries are consumers of processed materials and fabricated parts rather than of raw materials. There has been a continuing shift toward latter-stage processing and the production of finished products, with the consequent increase in the variety and volume of demand for industrial products. Expansion of the apparel industry increases the demand for cloth, thread, and fasteners such as zippers, buttons, and snaps.

The fabricated metals industry has expanded in proximity to the primary metals industry. In turn metal fabricators increasingly demand new qualities of primary metals to meet their manufacturing needs. Unlike the lumber industry, starting with logs, the relatively advanced transportation equipment industry requires finished parts and assemblies for production and repair of motor vehicles, ships, and aircraft.

So it is that industrial expansion and manufacturing diversification produce economic progress in Alabama's changing economy.

Growth in Basic Services

OVER THE PAST TWO DECADES ALABAMA'S TRANSPORTATION, COMmunication, and public utility facilities and services have grown at a rate exceeding that for the state's economy as a whole. This is understandable. It has often been observed that as an economy becomes more urban, more industrial, more commercial, and more prosperous the relative importance of all services, including those under discussion, tends to increase. In part these changes have been effects and to a lesser extent causes of the developments in agriculture, industry, and commerce that are being considered in this study.

The rapid development of highway freight transportation may be seen in the increase of payrolls generated in this field. Since 1939 the rate of growth of these payrolls in Alabama has exceeded the rate of rise in total personal income in the state. Furthermore, the published figures, favorable as they are, appear to understate the real payroll importance of motor freight transportation in Alabama. These data do not appear to include carriage of freight by business enterprises in their own or leased trucks. Consequently, a part of the payrolls of industrial and commercial enterprises other than common and contract motor carriers may also be attributed to the performance of transportation services. Although no complete figures are available, private carriage of this sort appears also to have grown more rapidly in recent years than has the Alabama economy as a whole.

Other direct and indirect transportation payrolls and hence market effects can be inferred from if not specifically measured by the increase in the physical volume of gasoline sold in the state in 1959 as compared with 1939. The increase was over fourfold—somewhat in excess of the real over-all growth in Alabama's economy. In the same period motor vehicle registrations have considerably more than tripled, and travel by out-of-state vehicles has grown rapidly. This situation explains the substantial growth of employment in connection with the operation of automobile sales establishments, repair garages, automotive parts establishments, service stations, motels, road machinery sales and repair establishments, road construction operations, and the road material supply business. The provision of new buildings and structures in connection with these operations also has stimulated employment in the construction industries.

Increased use of gasoline is not only a rough index of the growth of transportation-connected employment in our largest transportation sector, street and highway transportation, but it is also a good indicator of the use of personal transportation by individuals. It gives meaning to the term Transportation Revolution. This refers to the propensity of individuals, observed over several decades, to use more personal transportation and to enjoy it through the use of privately-owned automobiles. New demand for the services of the privately-owned automobile grows constantly because of its many advantages in this era of freeways, limited access interstate highways, and decentralized urban living.

In summary then it may be said that transportation as a whole, commercial, private business, and personal, has been a front runner in terms of growth in volume of service rendered and payrolls directly and indirectly created during the past twenty years. This is true even though growth in the rail sector of the transportation field has not been spectacular. Because of increased mechanization of the railroad industry, payroll growth has been modest. Nevertheless, growth of freight service has nearly kept pace with the expansion of the economy of the state.

The growth in volume of transportation services has been accompanied by many changes and improvements in the transportation agencies and facilities as well as in the quality of services available in Alabama.

Large railroads such as the Atlantic Coast Line, the Illinois Central, the Louisville and Nashville, the Seaboard Air Line, and the Southern Railway System have served Alabama for many years. Twenty years ago the creation of the Gulf Mobile and Ohio Railroad Company established a large new system which now provides Alabama business and industry with another single-company route to Chicago and St. Louis. Another interregional single-line route from the Port of Mobile to the Southwest and the Mississippi valley was established several years ago when the St. Louis and San Francisco Railroad Company acquired the Alabama, Tennessee and Northern Railroad Company.

The capacity of these carriers to render fast and flexible service has grown tremendously in the last two decades through the improvement of tracks, bridges, communications, the use of diesel power, the establishment of very efficient new freight classification yards, and other modern terminal facilities. The development of many new types of equipment such as facilities for combined rail-motor carriage has greatly increased the flexibility of railroad service.

Water transportation in Alabama during the past two decades also has shown great development.

Exports through the Port of Mobile rose from 887,000 tons in 1939 to 1,977,000 tons in 1959. During the same period imports increased from 611,000 tons to 7,690,000 tons. This latter figure reflects, among other things, the large quantities of iron ore now being brought in from South America by the iron and steel industry of the state.

GROWTH IN BASIC SERVICES 75

The Tennessee River flows within Alabama for a distance of nearly 200 miles. Traffic on this river increased from 2,163,000 tons in 1945 to 12,037,000 tons in 1959. Most of this traffic growth came after the nine-foot channel was completed and opened to navigation over its full length in 1948.

In its improved state the Tennessee River has played an important part in changing the economy of North Alabama. Within recent years several large corporations have established new plants in the area. Industries continue to show interest in the area because of low-cost water transportation, ample water and power supplies, and extensive recreational facilities.

The Warrior-Tombigbee river system, extending from Mobile on the Gulf of Mexico to Birmingham (Birmingport), has been described as "one of the busiest and fastest-growing inland barge channels in the Southeast." Traffic on this system has increased from 1,492,000 tons in 1945 to 5,756,000 tons in 1959.

Following World War II an intensified program of modernization of the Warrior-Tombigbee river system was undertaken. In 1954 old Locks 4, 5, 6, and 7 were replaced by a single-lift lock at Demopolis. Locks 8 and 9 were replaced by the Warrior Lock and Dam in 1958, and Locks 1, 2, and 3 were replaced in late 1960 by Jackson Lock and Dam near Coffeeville. Recently work was begun on Holt Lock and Dam which will replace Locks 13, 14, 15, and 16.

The continuing development of the Warrior-Tombigbee river system greatly improves the water supply as well as transportation along its course. Vast quantities of water that periodically used to flow unregulated to the sea are now impounded in a continuous series of man-made lakes created by the navigational dams. Further control of these abundant waters will come from dams on the headwaters of the river system, the first of which, a 300-foot-high hydro-electric power dam, was recently completed on the Sipsey Fork. This created a 21,000-acre lake that both reduces flood danger and creates a more even flow of water for industrial and domestic uses along the rivers.

It has been estimated that since 1955 more than $330,000,000 have been spent by industry for new and enlarged plant facilities along the Warrior-Tombigbee river system. This is exclusive of outlays for improvements to public utilities, recreational facilities, and transportation.

The planning is well along for canalization of the Alabama-Coosa River from its confluence with the Mobile River, north of Mobile, to Montgomery, with prospects of extending the navigable system to Gadsden.

A project is being developed to connect the Tombigbee River from its present head of navigation in Mississippi with the Tennessee River at Pickwick Dam. This will provide an inland water route from the upper Mississippi-Missouri, the Ohio, and the Tennessee Rivers through Mississippi and Alabama to Mobile. This project has Congressional authorization, but construction money has not been appropriated.

Canalization work is underway to extend navigation on the Chattahoochee River from the present head of navigation in the vicinity of Eufaula to Phenix City (Columbus, Georgia).

Although the waterways developments summarized here have already contributed much to the growth of the economy of Alabama, their impact will continue to be felt far into the future.

Great changes continue to be made in the capacity and efficiency of the highway system in Alabama. A large network of improved farm-to-market roads has been developed. The design and engineering of highway rights of way and structures has been greatly improved during the last two decades. In addition to the many miles of primary highway that have been built or improved many time-saving by-pass highways have also been constructed. When the new interstate system in Alabama is completed within the next few years, the principal highways of Alabama will be able to handle many times the traffic accommodated in 1940.

In the past twenty years commercial trucking in Alabama has grown into a mature and efficient industry fully adequate to meet the growing demands for motor transportation service. Many motor freight lines have been established in Alabama.

GROWTH IN BASIC SERVICES

Some Alabama-based companies as a group provide flexible and rather complete service within the state. They have built many new terminals throughout the state in recent years. Some of these companies together with others also offer region-wide service. A number of other Alabama-based companies offer inter-regional service between Alabama and the East, Mid-West, and Southwest. Several non-Alabama-based inter-regional and national carriers also serve the state. As a consequence industrial and commercial establishments in small towns and rural areas have access to quick and efficient local and long distance motor transportation. This has been a factor in the decentralized growth of our finished-product industries and distribution enterprises.

The other side of this picture is the increased ability of outside business interests to secure good service into the state. Recently a New York importer of fine food delicacies and confections who noted a growing demand for his products in a number of Alabama towns and cities was able to establish quick, low-cost service for medium and small sized shipments through the combined services of two Alabama-based motor carriers. One of these carriers had a New York-Alabama route, while the other offered local service to a large number of Alabama towns and cities.

In 1940 four certificated air carriers—Delta Air Corporation, Eastern Air Lines, Inc., National Airlines, Inc., and Pennsylvania-Central Airline Corporation—provided trunk-line service between Alabama and several sections of the country. Combined assets of these four organizations amounted to about $15,000,000. The first three of these concerns still serve our state under their original or similar names. The Pennsylvania-Central Airline Corporation became Capital Airlines, Inc., in 1948 and in 1961 merged with United Air Lines, Inc. Through this merger the services of the nation's largest air line became directly available to the Alabama community. At the present time single-company service is available between Alabama and the principal industrial, financial, commercial, and cultural centers of the United States.

In 1960 combined assets of trunk air lines then serving the state amounted to more than $1,100,000,000. This remarkable seventy-five-fold increase in the assets of air lines reaching our state cannot be used as an actual measure of the growth of service available to Alabama. However, it does testify to the fact that equipment is better and faster, that schedules are more frequent, that many more cities are hours nearer to Alabama than they were twenty years ago, and the quantity, extent, flexibility, and quality of service have been vastly improved.

Another air transportation service that has been a distinct aid to individuals, businesses, and other organizations in Alabama did not exist in the state two decades ago: local air line service such as is provided by Southern Airways. This service fulfills transportation needs arising from the growing community of interest among the many middle-sized cities of our state and area and between these urban units and the large urban centers in the Southeast. In Alabama local service is now available at Florence, Sheffield, Tuscumbia, Decatur, Huntsville, Anniston, Gadsden, Birmingham, Tuscaloosa, Selma, Dothan, and Mobile.

Another very important change in the transportation background of Alabama during the past two decades has been invisible and intangible but very substantial in its economic significance. It relates to the improvement of the freight rate position of Alabama and the South.

For many years the South was an area of amazing contrasts in freight rates. Most finished products and consumer goods carried very high freight rates. The rates were often 30 to 40 per cent higher per mile than rates on similar products moving in the North and East. Originally some differential was justifiable because the volume of this kind of traffic handled in the South was much lower in terms of the transportation plant doing the job than was the case in the North and the East. Unit costs were higher, consequently rates had to be higher. It was argued that the volume of this traffic could not be increased by lowering rates since it was the opinion of many that the only way to increase the movement of finished products and consumer goods

GROWTH IN BASIC SERVICES 79

on southern railroads was through a rise in the income and consuming power of the southern region. Consequently, the rates remained high relative to those in the North and East.

In the meantime, despairing of quickly increasing the volume of finished products and consumer goods traffic, the southern railroads sought ways of employing their unutilized capacity. As other parts of the country grew industrially they began to take an increasing interest in the raw materials and semi-processed products of Alabama and the South. The railroads of the South were interested in this development because it would provide new business for them. Since raw materials from Alabama would have to compete in other sections with local resources, freight rates from Alabama and the South would have to be low to produce a volume of traffic that would benefit the southern railroads. Hence, special low developmental rates, called commodity rates, were made applicable to these movements.

Thanks in part to this freight-rate-encouraged growth in the movement to other regions of raw and semi-processed materials, and in part to many other factors, Alabama and the South continued to grow economically. Railroad traffic increased. However, rates on consumer goods and many finished products (the class rates) remained at a higher level in the South than in the East.

Toward the end of the decade of the thirties various groups began to allege that the levels of class rates on which most consumer goods and some other finished products moved were not as fully justified as they were originally. They pointed to conditions that were lowering transportation costs in the South and raising them in the East. They claimed that it was becoming increasingly difficult on a cost basis to justify differences between the class-rate levels in the South and those in the East.

In addition they pointed to the low rates on raw materials and some semi-processed items and at the consequent ease with which these commodities could move out of Alabama and the South. Then they pointed out how difficult it was for southern producers of certain valuable finished products, even though they were very efficient, to market their wares in the North and East. Not only were they farther from the markets than their competitors in these regions, but they had to pay a higher rate per mile on the same commodities.

In the decades of the forties and fifties this situation was remedied. Class rates in the South were lowered somewhat and those in the East were raised. At present, with some exceptions, the class-rate levels in the South and the East and between these regions are now uniform. Today there is no artificial class-rate barrier to discourage efficient Alabama producers of consumer goods and high value finished products in their efforts to sell more of their output in other states and regions. This, then, is one important factor among many that have stimulated the growing diversity and the better balance and pattern of industry in the state, thus increasing the contribution of industry to the rising per capita income in Alabama.

During the past two decades public utility services in Alabama have enjoyed a faster rate of growth than that experienced by the over-all economy of the state. Facilities have been greatly expanded and improved, and the high quality of the services has been maintained.

Between 1939 and 1959 installed capacity of electric generating plants in Alabama increased from less than 1,000,000 kilowatts to more than 4,000,000 kilowatts. Kilowatt hours of electricity rose from about four billion to about twenty-three billion.

While manufactured gas has been available in Alabama for many years, the rapidly expanding natural gas distribution industry has been a phenomenon of recent decades. It has revolutionized the gas business and has been a tremendous aid to industrial growth and the home development business. On the basis of figures available, it seems reasonable to estimate that sales of natural and manufactured gas increased about six-fold between 1940 and 1960.

Though the increase in the population of Alabama has been rather modest during the past two decades, there has been a virtual explosion in the telephone service available to the people

GROWTH IN BASIC SERVICES 81

of the state. Telephones in use in 1940 numbered 133,000. By 1959 a total of 703,000 telephones had been installed. Not only was the number of telephones greatly increased but, as is self-evident, the communication potential of each phone was considerably enhanced.

The effect of the expansion of the telephone industry on payrolls in the state also has been outstanding. During the period under discussion wage payments in this industry increased from just over $3,000,000 to nearly $31,500,000.

The purpose of the foregoing discussion has been to indicate some of the changes in the transportation and utility service areas that have occurred during the past two decades of economic revolution in Alabama. The following points have been made:

1. Expansion in the volume of these basic services has more than kept up with the growth of the economy of Alabama. This is as it should be. In an economy that is becoming more sophisticated, more diverse, and more productive, increased use of transportation, power, fuel, and communications is necessary.

2. Developing transportation and utilities agencies have not merely served the economic revolution—they have stimulated its growth. In responding to the demands of a changing Alabama economy they have created jobs and markets. Not only have the direct and indirect payroll effects counted heavily in the growth of demand for consumer goods but also the capital investment has greatly increased the volume and influenced the character of demand for producer goods in Alabama.

3. Our modern systems of highways and waterways; our for-hire motor carriers, air lines, and railroads; and our communications and utilities agencies reflect innovations in technology, organization, and co-ordination. They not only have expanded rapidly to meet the past needs of the businesses and citizens of Alabama but also have increased their ability to render better and more flexible service in the future.

4. The disappearance of artificial freight rate barriers has given full play to the influence of transportation as a factor in improving the versatility and productivity of Alabama industry and commerce.

PART IV: THE MARKETING STRUCTURE

Wholesale Trade

THE ECONOMIC AND SOCIAL CHANGES IN ALABAMA HAVE BEEN ACcompanied by a changing marketing structure to meet new and changing demands. The increase in the percentage of our people living in urban areas has brought about a different way of living, causing new buying patterns and new needs. The marketing structure has met the task of providing more people with a higher standard of living by becoming more like the marketing structures of other urban states. Shopping centers stand on edges of cities in areas that were forests or farms a few short years ago. Towns that were once small agricultural trading centers now have become industrially oriented, depending on wages rather than unpredictable farm income. The wholesale districts of our large cities have been relocated, often in outlying areas, for the purpose of employing more efficient methods in the physical handling of goods. As Alabama has become more industrially oriented, new marketing structures have been developed and old marketing structures have been adapted to provide distribution channels for goods produced in Alabama. The marketing structure has become more efficient.

Alabama has developed dramatically as a wholesaling center during the past twenty years. Dollar wholesale sales in 1958 ($2,853,000,000) were nearly seven times the 1939 level ($416,000,000). Alabama's percentage of total United States wholesale sales increased by one-third between 1939 and 1958, compared with an increase of one-fourth in its portion of retail sales. Changes in retail sales are associated with changes in population and income while changes in wholesale sales are affected by the growth of market centers and the development of industrial and commercial users of goods sold through wholesale channels. It appears that commercial and industrial development as represented by wholesale markets has at least kept up with the rapidly developing retail economy in Alabama.

Other evidence of the increasing importance of Alabama as a wholesale market is its substantially greater rate of growth in number of establishments and employment in wholesaling. Between 1939 and 1958 the number of wholesale establishments in Alabama increased by 75 per cent in contrast with a 43 per cent increase in the nation. In the ten-year period, 1948 to 1958, employment in wholesaling in Alabama increased 26 per cent while it was increasing 17 per cent in the nation.

Birmingham is the wholesaling center of the state. Since 1948 Birmingham (Jefferson County) has accounted for more than 50 per cent of Alabama's wholesale sales. In contrast, it has been responsible for about 25 per cent of the state's retail sales. Mobile County has consistently had about 11 per cent of both wholesale and retail sales. In 1958 8 per cent of the wholesale sales and 6.5 per cent of the retail sales were in Montgomery County. Etowah County (Gadsden) had 1.10 per cent of the state's wholesale sales and 3.15 per cent of the state's retail sales. Even though the figures show that the state's three most populous urban counties are responsible for over 70 per cent of the state's wholesale sales, it is significant that no county in Alabama has less than three wholesaling establishments.

One measure of the relative development of wholesaling within an area is the ratio of wholesale to retail sales. The ratio

TABLE 10. RATIOS OF WHOLESALE TO RETAIL SALES,
ALABAMA CITIES, 1939, 1948, 1954, AND 1958

City	1939	1948	1954	1958
Birmingham	1.53	1.92	2.26	2.20
Montgomery	1.77	1.73	1.33	1.41
Mobile	1.23	1.03	1.14	1.08

Source: *U. S. Census of Business,* 1939, 1948, and 1958 (BC 58-WA1 and BC 58-RA1).

for the United States was 1.31 in 1939 and 1.43 in 1958. The Alabama ratio was 1.11 in 1958 compared with .95 in 1939. The relationship for Alabama cities is shown in Table 10. Ratios for other southeastern cities for 1958 were: New Orleans 2.58, Atlanta 3.25, and Jacksonville 2.60.

The structure of wholesaling in Alabama was more like the national structure in 1958 than it was in 1939. (Table 11.) The decline in relative importance of merchant wholesalers in Alabama brought the state in line with a relatively stable national picture. The trend towards the increasing importance of manufacturers' sales branches was not as consistent in Alabama as nationally. Petroleum bulk plants represent a larger portion of the wholesaling structure in Alabama than in the United States. Merchandise agents and brokers have not yet achieved the importance in the state that they have nationally. Agents and brokers are active in certain special industries which are not as important in Alabama markets as elsewhere. With the sharp decline in the number of small farms, assemblers of farm products have become less significant both nationally and in the state.

In the merchant wholesaler group, grocery wholesalers lost ground in Alabama with their sales declining from 30.95 per cent in 1948 to 21.04 per cent of the group total in 1958. This was very near the national figure of 20.71 per cent in 1958. The trend may be partially explained by a larger proportion of the food business being handled by large direct-buying chain and independent-merchant groups. The greatest gains in relative importance were made in the furniture and home furnishings field (from .39 per cent of total merchant wholesaler sales in 1948 to 1.38 per cent in 1958), in the automotive field (from 3.20 to

TABLE 11. WHOLESALING STRUCTURE, ALABAMA AND THE UNITED STATES, 1939, 1948, 1954, AND 1958
(Sales in millions of dollars)

Type of wholesaler	Year	Alabama		United States	
		Sales	Per cent of total	Sales	Per cent of total
Merchant wholesalers	1939	209	50.24	23,642	42.78
	1948	783	46.66	79,767	42.27
	1954	1,011	43.63	100,102	42.78
	1958	1,304	45.71	121,661	42.69
Manufacturers' sales branches, offices	1939	88	21.15	13,526	24.47
	1948	447	26.64	52,739	27.95
	1954	740	31.94	69,534	29.72
	1958	800	28.04	87,757	30.80
Petroleum bulk plants, terminals	1939	47	11.30	3,808	6.89
	1948	151	9.00	10,615	5.63
	1954	240	10.36	16,038	6.85
	1958	321	11.25	20,131	7.06
Merchandise agents, brokers	1939	51	12.26	11,201	20.27
	1948	198	11.80	34,610	18.34
	1954	268	11.57	39,251	16.78
	1958	344	12.06	46,423	16.29
Assemblers of farm products	1939	21	5.05	3,089	5.59
	1948	99	5.90	10,958	5.81
	1954	58	2.50	9,051	3.87
	1958	84	2.94	8,999	3.16
Total	1939	416	100.00	55,266	100.00
	1948	1,678	100.00	188,689	100.00
	1954	2,317	100.00	233,976	100.00
	1958	2,853	100.00	284,971	100.00

Source: *U. S. Census of Business,* 1939, 1948, and 1958 (BC 58-WA2).

WHOLESALE TRADE

6.24 per cent), and in metals and metalwork (.35 to 2.71 per cent). The greatest declines were in lumber and construction materials (10.04 to 6.62 per cent) and in scrap and waste materials (5.04 to 3.97 per cent).

In each instance the trend has brought Alabama closer to the national pattern. The change in proportion of sales of automotive wholesalers and metals and metalwork wholesalers is especially significant when compared with the trend in the national percentages (automotive 5.13 to 5.83, metals and metalwork 2.58 to 3.80). These figures seem to be in line with increased industrialization and a higher standard of living.

Retail Trade

THE SIX-FOLD INCREASE IN DOLLAR VALUE OF RETAIL SALES IN ALAbama from 1939 to 1958 gave the state a 25 per cent increase in its share of retail sales in the nation. (Table 12.)

TABLE 12. ALABAMA AS A PERCENTAGE OF UNITED STATES: RETAIL SALES, POPULATION, PERSONAL INCOME, AND PER CAPITA INCOME, SELECTED YEARS, 1939 TO 1960

Year	Alabama's percentage of United States			
	Retail sales	Population	Personal income	Per capita income
1939	1.04	......	.97	44.96
1940	......	2.15	1.02	47.39
1948	1.26	......	1.23	62.80
1950	......	2.03	1.18	58.15
1954	1.24	......	1.14	60.34
1958	1.29	......	1.22	54.89
1960	......	1.83	1.20	65.92

Sources: *U. S. Census of Business*, 1939, 1954, and 1958 (BC 58-RA1); *U. S. Census of Population*, 1940, 1950, and 1960; *Personal Income by States Since 1929*, a supplement to the *Survey of Current Business*, 1956; *Survey of Current Business*, August, 1961.

RETAIL TRADE

The quality of Alabama's retail market is improving. Alabama's portion of the nation's personal income has been increasing while its portion of the nation's population has been declining. As a result per capita income of Alabamians has increased nearly 40 per cent relative to the national average during the past two decades. (Table 12.) Moreover, Alabamians tend to spend a greater share of their income in retail stores than do people in the nation as a whole.

The pattern of retail sales in Alabama is becoming more like that for the nation. The most notable difference is in the relative importance of eating and drinking places. (Table 13.) Out of every $100 spent at retail in the United States in 1958, $7.60 was spent in eating and drinking places; whereas in Alabama this expenditure was only $4.60. There are three other notable differences. In 1958 Alabamians spent more in the general merchandise and the automotive groups and less in the non-store retailers group than did the national population. On the other hand, almost identical portions of the retail sales dollar were spent in the food, the lumber-building-hardware, and the drug stores business groups in both Alabama and the nation.

Changes in the pattern of retail sales in Alabama between 1948 and 1958 were not great except in two groups. Expenditures in service stations rose from $5.30 to $7.70 per hundred dollars of retail sales while those in general merchandise stores declined from $15.10 to $12.80 per hundred dollars of sales. This decline in importance of general merchandise stores is largely the result of the decline in the rural population of the state, and hence in sales through country general stores.

The largest gain in dollar volume of retail sales was the $228,000,000 increase in the food group sales, an increase of 56 per cent. The automotive group was second with a 54 per cent increase of $158,000,000. In third place were service stations, whose sales increased $111,000,000, a gain of 129 per cent.

The largest percentage increase, 303 per cent, was in the sales of non-store retailers which rose from $8,000,000 to $32,000,000. This group is composed of mail-order houses, vending machines, and direct selling (house-to-house) organizations, the last representing over two-thirds of the group total in 1958. As might be expected, the smallest percentage increase in sales, 34 per cent, was in the general merchandise group.

About 50 per cent of Alabama's retail sales consistently have been made in five (not always the same) leading counties. Jefferson County has consistently led with about one-fourth of all retail sales in the state.

TABLE 13. RETAIL TRADE, BY KIND OF BUSINESS GROUP, ALABAMA, AND PERCENTAGE DISTRIBUTION OF RETAIL TRADE, ALABAMA AND UNITED STATES, 1948 AND 1958

Kind of business	Sales ($1,000)		Net change 1948 to 1958		Percentage distribution			
					Alabama		United States	
	1948	1958	Sales ($1,000)	Per cent	1948	1958	1948	1958
Food	407,468	635,096	227,628	55.9	25.0	24.7	22.7	24.6
General merchandise	246,054	329,621	83,567	34.0	15.1	12.8	12.3	11.0
Apparel	114,240	169,803	55,563	48.6	7.0	6.6	7.5	6.3
Furniture-household-radio	89,798	139,480	49,682	55.3	5.5	5.4	5.1	5.0
Automotive	292,924	451,124	158,200	54.0	18.0	17.6	15.6	15.9
Service stations	86,094	196,923	110,829	128.7	5.3	7.7	5.0	7.1
Lumber-building-hardware	117,306	180,986	63,680	54.3	7.2	7.1	8.6	7.2
Eating and drinking places	82,579	116,942	34,363	41.6	5.1	4.6	8.3	7.6
Drug stores	50,533	89,344	38,811	76.8	3.1	3.5	3.1	3.4
Other stores	133,729	226,218	92,489	69.2	8.2	8.8	10.0	9.2
Nonstore retailers	7,860	31,700	23,840	303.3	.5	1.2	1.8	2.7
Total	1,628,585	2,567,237	938,652	57.6	100.0	100.0	100.0	100.0

Source: *U. S. Census of Business*, 1954, 1958.

Highlights of the Study

This is a transcript from tape of a summary presented orally by the Coördinator to the Research Committee before some data for 1960 became available, hence the reference to 1959 data.

THESE ARE A FEW OF THE HIGHLIGHTS OF THIS SURVEY. THEY DO NOT cover more than a fourth of the things that we have tabulated. They are just some of the things that I think would attract attention, for instance, on a news program. Some of them are literally sensational. There is nothing original about them. This sensationalism is due to the facts and not to any genius on the part of the research staff.

It just happens that this is a most interesting time to study the economic changes in the State of Alabama.

In my undergraduate life in a course in geology I learned that you have stresses and strains in the earth's crust for a long time—maybe for years, maybe for centuries, maybe for eons—then you get something like an earthquake or the breakout of a volcano. Similarly, in social life long-term stresses and strains eventually cause a sudden change in the nature of a community.

We are passing such a point in Alabama at the present time as you will see from these highlights. They have all been in the newspapers, but the public has not put them together, has not interpreted them as yet, so that the people do not realize that we are just going through, or have just gone through, some of the most momentous changes that have ever happened to the society in which we live.

Alabama is now an urban state. Twenty years ago its population was about 70 per cent rural. Now, by the same definition, it is only 48.3 per cent rural, and by the Census Bureau's new definition it is but 45.2 per cent rural. Of the households only 42.5 per cent are rural. More than a third (36.1 per cent) of the total population live in six urbanized places and part of another.[1]

The people of Alabama have made vast gains in income. They had $700,000,000 of income in 1939 when our period of study began and in 1959 they had $4,600,000,000 of income. That is a five and one-half fold increase for Alabama compared to a four-fold increase for the nation. This is the most impressive thing about the income changes and about the whole market aspect of our economy.

To put it another way, Alabama's cut of the national income came up from 0.97 per cent to 1.21 per cent. That doesn't sound very big; a change of just twenty-four hundredths. But let's look at it this way:

I like to think of national income as a great big lemon pie with golden brown meringue on top. This national pie has become five times as thick as it was and our slice is one-fourth wider.

Per capita income is up from $250 to $1,420 in that twenty years, so the Alabama market is rich and growing. We haven't passed any states through the years; we are in the same rank among the states that we were in 1929. We had three states under us then. Now we have three states under us—the same three.

But here is where we have made progress. We had only 45

[1] Phenix City, adjoined to Columbus, Georgia.

HIGHLIGHTS OF THE STUDY

per cent of the national per capita income in 1939. Now we have 66 per cent. You see what has been happening. All industrialists are familiar with the closing of the gap between grades of labor. There has been a closing of the gap between the states incomewise. To put it another way, Delaware, the richest state in both 1939 and 1959, had in 1939 nearly four times as much per capita income as Alabama. It now has just twice as much.

Alabama's is a wage-earning economy and increasingly so. In 1939 wages and salaries made up 62.5 per cent of the total income. In 1959 they made up 67.5 per cent. Where did that increase come from? Out of income from property and proprietorship, including corporate ownership. Understand that proprietors' income increased several fold, but so much less than wages and salaries that its share of total income dropped from 23.7 per cent in 1939 to 14.9 per cent in 1959. The property income share declined from 10.4 per cent to 8.8 per cent over the decade.

Most of the decline in proprietors' share of income was in farm proprietors' income which dropped from 13.5 per cent twenty years ago to 5.2 per cent. To be exact, what farming contributes to the income of the people of Alabama is only 5.8 per cent when we include farm wages. What makes me so vehement about this is that I was in a bookstore downtown the other day and there was a beautiful book with a lot in it about Alabama. The chapter on Alabama was headed "The Cotton State"—just 1.5 per cent of the income of the people of Alabama is derived from raising cotton. I didn't see a cotton field between here and Montgomery the last time I drove down there. I did see this— beautiful green fields, as beautiful as I ever saw in hill country, even in northwest Wisconsin. I thought, up until then, that those Wisconsin hills were the prettiest hill country that I ever saw cultivated. Flat countries are easy to cultivate but the hills you have to terrace. We have some farmers who are real farmers, but more of that later.

The point is that here are two markets; one is half as rich as the other, but the poorer market is growing a great deal faster than the richer market. Aren't they both awfully good markets from the point of view of the sales manager? That is the case with Alabama and some of the other states. They have more income there now, but we are gaining faster, have been gaining faster for twenty years, and there is every evidence that we are still gaining faster.

Even though this is a wage-earning economy now, the farm market in Alabama is improving. I don't say it is growing, but it is changing and improving. Farms are getting fewer, bigger, more owner-operated, and require bigger investments. Now I think one of the best products of this Council was the study *Flight From the Soil.* I know of no better original study about the reasons for people leaving the farm than this study of 700 people who left the farm in Alabama and the reasons why they left, what kind of people they were before they left, under what conditions they would go back, and all that.

You don't have to add a thing to that study to bring it up to date, for we note a continuance of the same things that were reported there. In the five years between the agricultural censuses of 1954 and 1959 the number of farms in Alabama dropped from 177,000 to 116,000. *More than one-fourth of all farms dropped out in five years.* Fourteen thousand of these dropouts are accounted for by a change in the definition of farm, but it is my opinion that the current definition is still over-generous in defining a person as a farmer and I feel confident that probably even more real farmers left the farm in those five years.

The average size of farm in Alabama has risen from 117 to 143 acres—still small when compared with farms in the best farming areas. The average value of land and buildings is up from $6,200 to $11,800. Some types of farming in Alabama now require an investment 50 per cent more than the average investment to employ a man in industry.

The use of the land is changing rapidly and dramatically. Crops are lessening in importance and pastures and forests are gaining. In driving back from Montgomery recently I saw little cultivated planting, even around the houses. But what I did see were pine trees, pine trees, pine trees—just miles and

HIGHLIGHTS OF THE STUDY 95

miles of them. Not everywhere, but some pine trees always in sight, sometimes little patches of them, sometimes 50 acres or more of them. As you get back off the main roads, which are more cleared, the plantings of pine trees are even thicker. So many previously almost unused acres are now in pines producing lumber and pulpwood for the rapidly growing paper industry.

The number of acres in farms fell 20 per cent in five years but gross farm income has risen some because of more efficient use of the fewer acres.

According to the Census classification, there were in 1959 a little less than 30,000 cotton farms in the state and there were 16,000 livestock farms, counting chicken farms, dairy farms, and so on. There were more than half as many livestock farms as there were cotton farms.

The commercial farmers produced most of the products. There were not many of them, 33,000 whose sales came to more than $2,500 a year. Thirty-three thousand; that is all. If you are selling to farmers—selling fertilizer, selling feed, implements, or anything—you have only 33,000 farmers who sell more than $2,500 worth of products a year to go to. Now there were another 24,000 who were classed as Commercial VI by the Census. Their main living was from farming but they sold less than $2,500 worth of products. They are what the study, *Flight From the Soil,* called marginal farmers. I think all of these farmers with sales of less than $2,500 are candidates for Gadsden, Tuscaloosa, or some mill town.

Now 57,700 of the total of 115,600 farmers in Alabama are classified as commercial farmers. The other 58,000 are classified as part-time farmers. The definition has been changed some from that used in *Flight From the Soil.* This second group of 58,000 farmers all worked 100 days or more off the farm. They live on the farm but few of them get their major income from farming.

Tenancy has gone out. Our forefathers learned during the time of reconstruction how to finance cotton and tobacco crops by mortgaging the crop. It was the only way they could have done it that I can think of. They reconstituted the cotton plantation system on that basis. From that time until now this has been a tenant-farming state, but in the past five years Alabama ceased to be a tenant-farming state. One-half of the tenants dropped out. There were 61,000 tenants enumerated in the 1954 Census, 32,000 in 1959. Now, gentlemen, here is a prediction on which you can't lose: tenants cannot leave the farms of Alabama at the same rate until the end of 1965 that they left the farms from 1954 to 1959. We would run out of tenants before then.

Wholesaling is gaining rapidly in Alabama. I used to teach my classes about twenty-five or thirty years ago that merchant wholesalers were on their way out and gave examples. I had evidence if anybody wanted to argue with me; all the big wholesalers in Alabama except about three or four had gone broke right before my eyes. But there is not a county in Alabama today that does not have at least three wholesalers and the typical county has eight, ten, or a dozen. These merchant wholesalers in 1958 sold about a billion and one-third dollars worth of goods. These fellows that the big retailers and chain stores had put out of business about a generation ago are back. All wholesalers, including brokers, agents, assemblers, etc., had sales amounting to nearly $3,000,000,000 in 1958.

Alabama is generally considered to be a mineral state. Everybody seems to think that we make a living from raising cotton and mining coal and iron. It is a mineral state, but not an important one. Alabama's production of coal reached a peak in 1926 and of iron ore in 1942. Production of both gained in 1960 over 1959, but coal in 1960 was 40 per cent below the peak in 1926 and iron ore was 48 per cent below the peak in 1942.

The value of minerals produced in Alabama in 1959 was just barely under $200,000,000. The top four minerals in the order of value were: coal, cement, stone, and iron ore.

In 1960 the value of minerals produced rose to $208,000,000. The top five minerals in order of value were: coal, cement, stone, iron ore, and petroleum. Petroleum production in 1960

HIGHLIGHTS OF THE STUDY

was valued at $22,000,000. It is catching up with iron ore. The iron mines in the state that year produced $26,000,000 worth of ore and imports fell to $23,000,000 worth.

The total production of minerals and mineral products in Alabama in 1959 was 1.17 per cent of the national production of minerals. Now remember that our income in the same year amounted to 1.21 per cent of the national total and you can see that minerals do not tote their part of the load. It is the business activities that are bringing up Alabama's income: they represent that half of the income that comes from retailing, wholesaling, banking, insurance, and a half dozen other activities that produce more income than cotton farming does.

We import a lot of things besides iron ore. The total value of metallic raw and semi-processed materials brought into Mobile in 1960 was $64,000,000. That was just a trifle more than half of all the imports.

We begin to see better what kind of an economy we now have in Alabama. When I came here nearly fifty years ago and began to study the Alabama economy, it was a farming economy supplemented by extractive industry. Then we shipped out raw and semi-processed materials. Now we not only use our own but import others as well—tin metal in crude and semi-fabricated forms, crude rubber, manganese, iron ore and concentrates, bauxite, and fertilizer materials.

Alabama no longer has a raw, primary, extractive economy. It is a more highly developed type of economy, similar to England or the Netherlands—more so than most of the American states. And it is not restricted to metals. We have two huge rubber factories in Alabama. Why are they here? Because we are convenient to sources of carbon black on this side of the ocean and to rubber through Mobile; $10,000,000 worth of raw rubber came from Southeast Asia last year.

We brought in a couple of million dollars worth of unmanufactured fibers—non-competitive with American fibers—sisal, henequen, jute. One plant, run by one of my former students in Mobile, is making up nearly all of it.

Raw materials and semi-manufactured products account for 65 per cent of Alabama's imports. Then there is a lot of food like bananas and other fruits but comparatively little manufactured products—the biggest item being about $4,000,000 worth of machinery, including automobiles, the biggest single item.

Now, that is not all. Even in agriculture we are doing the same kind of thing. We are making a better and better living out of bringing something in and using it with something we have in Alabama. We have labor, we have land, we have climate. So we bring in midwestern grain and feed it to chickens and cattle and sell it for several times as much per pound as the midwestern farmers got for it. It is an operation similar to the steel industry in Alabama.

The thing that enabled the southern states to take the chicken markets away from others was that before they started they learned how to feed antibiotics and growth-stimulating drugs of various kinds to the chickens. There was a limited number of people—an educated group of people—who understood the scientists' language and were willing to follow the scientists' advice.

Right now the thing that is growing fastest in the Alabama agricultural economy is converting midwestern grain into something very much more valuable. And since we got the jump on the know-how, I think we might keep a jump or two ahead on the operation.

I make this generalization. What we have now, in fact, is an established market—we know where we can sell. We have some or all of the raw materials used, but they may need supplementing or some enrichment, as in the case of iron ore. We have the know-how. We have colleges and universities turning out men with the latest ideas—developing men for managing, producing, selling, and making more effective use of the state's resources. We have reached the stage in the development of the economy of Alabama where brains and skill have taken over from brawn and inexperience.

I have had the privilege of reporting to you on one of the

most interesting and remarkable transitions in economic history which has put Alabama ahead of many states in the character of its economy. But the transition is not yet fully accomplished. As it proceeds, Alabama will continue to improve its position relative to the national economy.

APPENDIX

ALABAMA BUSINESS RESEARCH COUNCIL

MEMBERSHIP ROSTER, 1960-1961

ADVISORY COMMITTEE MEMBERS	RESEARCH COMMITTEE REPRESENTATIVES
Alexander City	
THE RUSSELL MANUFACTURING COMPANY	
THOMAS D. RUSSELL, PRESIDENT	J. L. COLEY, PERSONNEL DIRECTOR
Birmingham	
ALABAMA GAS CORPORATION	
JOSEPH N. GREENE, CHAIRMAN	NORMAN R. KERREDGE, TREASURER
ALABAMA POWER COMPANY	
WALTER BOULDIN, PRESIDENT	J. H. MILLER, JR., ASSISTANT TO THE PRESIDENT
AMERICAN CAST IRON PIPE COMPANY	
S. D. MOXLEY, PRESIDENT	JOHN G. FOSHEE, TREASURER
AMERICAN LIBERTY INSURANCE COMPANY	
FRED A. CARNELL, PRESIDENT	JOSEPH R. MOORE, VICE PRESIDENT
THE BIRMINGHAM NEWS AND POST-HERALD	
CLARENCE B. HANSON, JR., PUBLISHER	ROBERT P. HUNTER, SECRETARY-TREASURER *Vice-Chairman, Research Committee, Alabama Business Research Council*
BIRMINGHAM TRUST NATIONAL BANK	
FRANK A. PLUMMER, PRESIDENT	JOHN L. LILES, JR., VICE PRESIDENT
CHICAGO BRIDGE & IRON COMPANY	
A. G. SMITH, PLANT MANAGER	R. A. DAVIS, STAFF ENGINEER
JACK COLE COMPANY, INC.	
JOHN B. COLE, JR., PRESIDENT	
CONTINENTAL GIN COMPANY	
A. L. VANDERGRIFF, PRESIDENT	

APPENDIX

ADVISORY COMMITTEE MEMBERS	RESEARCH COMMITTEE REPRESENTATIVES
DEBARDELEBEN COAL CORPORATION	
Newton DeBardeleben, President	Alvin W. Vogtle, Vice President
EBSCO INDUSTRIES, INC.	
Elton B. Stephens, President	W. Oliver Cox, Director Select-A-Gift Program
EXCHANGE SECURITY BANK	
A. M. Shook, Chairman	Jack Alexander, Vice President
FIRST NATIONAL BANK OF BIRMINGHAM	
John A. Hand, President	Julian Mason, Vice President
THE HAYES INTERNATIONAL CORPORATION	
Lewis Jeffers, President	W. C. Hagan, Jr., Director of Industrial Relations
	D. J. Jones, Manager of Personnel
JEFFERSON FEDERAL SAVINGS AND LOAN ASSOCIATION	
F. B. Yeilding, Jr., President	Brooks Yeilding, Secretary
LIBERTY NATIONAL LIFE INSURANCE COMPANY	
Frank P. Samford, President	Harold H. Hays, Vice President
LOVEMAN, JOSEPH & LOEB	
Paul Dowd, President	John R. Lehman, Comptroller
ROBERT LUCKIE AND COMPANY, INC.	
Robert E. Luckie, Jr., President-Treasurer	
PROTECTIVE LIFE INSURANCE COMPANY	
William J. Rushton, President	Jay Vawter, Security Analyst
SOUTHERN BELL TELEPHONE AND TELEGRAPH COMPANY	
Frank Newton, Vice President and General Manager	Carl T. Happer, Jr., General Commercial Manager
	R. B. Knox, Jr., Division Commercial Engineer

ADVISORY COMMITTEE MEMBERS	RESEARCH COMMITTEE REPRESENTATIVES
SOUTHERN NATURAL GAS COMPANY	
C. Pratt Rather, President	Mortimer Jordan, Vice President and Director of Public Relations
TAFT BROADCASTING COMPANY, WBRC TV, RED MOUNTAIN	
R. T. Schlinkert, Local Manager	
TENNESSEE COAL & IRON DIVISION, UNITED STATES STEEL CORPORATION	
Arthur V. Wiebel, President	Earl W. Mallick, Staff Assistant, Executive Department Charles R. Knight, Manager, Commercial Research
VULCAN MATERIALS COMPANY	
B. A. Monaghan, President	C. A. Barinowski, Vice President

Decatur

THE CHEMSTRAND CORPORATION	
James H. Crow, Jr., Vice President	John Hard, Personnel Superintendent
DECATUR IRON & STEEL COMPANY	
J. F. Scroggins, President	John B. Wood, Personnel Director
WOLVERINE TUBE DIVISION OF CALUMET & HECLA, INC.	
H. E. Ross, Plant Manager	James B. Snider, Production Planning Supervisor Paul Blackwell, Industrial Engineering Supervisor
WORTHINGTON CORPORATION, DECATUR WORKS	
E. R. Maddock, Works Manager	W. S. Crawford, Personnel Manager

Florence

STYLON CORPORATION, FLORENCE OPERATION	
J. R. Sevier, Vice President	Noble L. Arnett, Personnel Director

APPENDIX

ADVISORY COMMITTEE MEMBERS	RESEARCH COMMITTEE REPRESENTATIVES
	Mobile
	ALUMINUM COMPANY OF AMERICA, ALABAMA OPERATIONS
CARR SMITH, WORKS MANAGER	LON B. MORELAND, PUBLIC RELATIONS MANAGER
	J. H. GOLDMAN, ASSISTANT PUBLIC RELATIONS MANAGER
	AMERICAN NATIONAL BANK AND TRUST COMPANY
GEORGE H. DENNISTON, PRESIDENT	HENRY WELLS, ASSISTANT VICE PRESIDENT
	DELCHAMPS, INC.
ALFRED DELCHAMPS, PRESIDENT	O. H. DELCHAMPS, JR., ASSISTANT TREASURER
	A. F. DELCHAMPS, JR., ASSISTANT SECRETARY
	INTERNATIONAL PAPER COMPANY
A. L. ROSS, VICE PRESIDENT	R. H. ALLEN, JR., ASSISTANT SECRETARY *Chairman, Research Committee, Alabama Business Research Council*
	JACK'S COOKIE COMPANY, INC.
JOHN W. BARTON, PRESIDENT	
	THE LERIO CORPORATION
WILLIAM B. WELCH, EXECUTIVE VICE PRESIDENT	
	THE MERCHANTS NATIONAL BANK OF MOBILE
J. F. MCRAE, PRESIDENT	E. G. CLEVERDON, SENIOR VICE PRESIDENT AND CASHIER
	SCOTT PAPER COMPANY, SOUTHERN DIVISION
JOHN W. MCNICHOL, GENERAL MANAGER	JAMES H. COIL, JR., MANAGER OF ADMINISTRATIVE SERVICES
	R. M. STEVENSON, MANAGER OF CONTRACTS, TAXES, AND INSURANCE
	Montgomery
	BLOUNT BROTHERS CONSTRUCTION COMPANY
WINTON M. BLOUNT, PRESIDENT	HOLMAN HEAD, DIRECTOR OF PERSONNEL

ADVISORY COMMITTEE MEMBERS *RESEARCH COMMITTEE REPRESENTATIVES*

FIRST NATIONAL BANK
Walter Kennedy, President   James S. Gaskell, Jr., Vice President

KERSHAW MANUFACTURING COMPANY
Royce Kershaw, President   E. E. Bode, Sales Manager

Sheffield

DIAMOND ALKALI COMPANY
M. C. Sullender, Plant Manager   John Whittleman, Personnel Manager

Sylacauga

AVONDALE MILLS, INC.
J. Craig Smith, President   Graham M. Byrum, Advertising and Sales Promotion Manager
B. H. Haynes, Personnel Manager

Tuscaloosa

THE FIRST NATIONAL BANK
Frank M. Moody, President   George Shirley, Assistant Vice President

B. F. GOODRICH COMPANY
F. N. Lehmann, Plant Manager

GULF STATES PAPER CORPORATION
J. W. Warner, President   Malcolm N. May, Manufacturing Manager

THE TUSCALOOSA NEWS
Buford Boone, Publisher   James Ward, Advertising Manager

APPENDIX

THE UNIVERSITY OF ALABAMA

FRANK A. ROSE, PRESIDENT

SCHOOL OF COMMERCE AND BUSINESS ADMINISTRATION
FACULTY ADVISORY COMMITTEE

LEE BIDGOOD
DEAN EMERITUS
Research Coördinator, Alabama Business Research Council

S. PAUL GARNER
DEAN

W. R. BENNETT
PROFESSOR OF MARKETING

HENRY B. MOORE
PROFESSOR OF ECONOMICS AND
DIRECTOR OF BUSINESS RESEARCH

PAUL W. PAUSTIAN
PROFESSOR OF ECONOMICS

CHARLES R. SCOTT
PROFESSOR OF MANAGEMENT

MARCUS WHITMAN
PROFESSOR OF FINANCE

Research Staff
JOSEPH B. WASHINGTON
RESEARCH ASSOCIATE

MRS. RUTH C. DUNN
SECRETARY

MRS. CHALMER GEORGE
STATISTICAL CLERK

ASSOCIATE MEMBER FIRMS

ALABAMA, TENNESSEE & NORTHERN
RAILROAD COMPANY
MOBILE, ALABAMA

ALLIS-CHALMERS MANUFACTURING
COMPANY
GADSDEN, ALABAMA

THE CENTRAL FOUNDRY COMPANY
TUSCALOOSA, ALABAMA

GENERAL ELECTRIC COMPANY
ANNISTON, ALABAMA

GOODYEAR TIRE & RUBBER COMPANY
OF ALABAMA
GADSDEN, ALABAMA

GULF, MOBILE AND OHIO RAILROAD
COMPANY
MOBILE, ALABAMA

MONTGOMERY ADVERTISER-ALABAMA
JOURNAL
MONTGOMERY, ALABAMA

REPUBLIC STEEL CORPORATION
GADSDEN, ALABAMA

REYNOLDS METALS COMPANY
SHEFFIELD, ALABAMA

W. T. SMITH LUMBER COMPANY
CHAPMAN, ALABAMA

STOCKHAM VALVES & FITTINGS
BIRMINGHAM, ALABAMA

WESTINGHOUSE ELECTRIC CORPORATION
BIRMINGHAM, ALABAMA

WIMBERLY & THOMAS HARDWARE
COMPANY, INC.
BIRMINGHAM, ALABAMA